Asad Zaman

Guardians of the Houses of Allah

Muslim American Society

Asad Zaman

Guardians of the Houses of Allah

Published by: Muslim American Society

Text Design by: Abdelminem Mustafa

A CIP record for this book is acailable from the Library of Congress Cataloging-in-Publication Data

ISBN: 978-0-9792113-2-4

This book is dedicated to the men and
women who support, organize, donate to,
and maintain the Houses of Allah.

I ask Allah to accept our services and gather
us together at the house where the angels
worship, *Al-Bayt al-Ma'moor*

Guardians of the Houses of Allah

ASAD ZAMAN

Contents

Preface

You are an amazing human being. You are a guardian of a house from among the houses of Allah. You are praised by our Lord as He describes your qualities in His eternal message.

By donating to a Masjid, by building, maintaining, improving or cleaning it, by joining the board of a Masjid, or by serving as an Imam, you have joined a very exclusive club, the Guardians of the Houses of Allah.

Not everyone can join this club. Entry criteria have to be met, and this club has ongoing membership requirements. Not everyone can maintain their membership in this club. This book seeks to describe the best practices of managing a masjid.

The idea for this book came to me over five years ago, but I hesitated for a long time to write this book. I hesitated because I feel I have neither perfected my own ṣalāh as a worshipper of Allah, nor have I accomplished the best practices of managing a masjid as a caretaker. My colleagues helped me overcome my reluctance by their repeated discussion of Masjid best practices. I thank them profusely for encouraging me to undertake this book.

I present this book as goals I aspire toward, not as accomplishments I have attained. Indeed, my personal ṣalāh is severely lacking. and the masjids I manage fall far short of the ideal masjid built by the noble Messenger ﷺ. I am not an authority on this subject and would not normally publish such a book. But the underlying need for a book on best practices of Masjid management continues to persist.

I ask Allah to accept this offering, despite its obvious defects. I hope it might be of some benefit to my fellow guardians of the houses of Allah.

Asad Zaman
Ramadan 1442
April 2021

Chapter 1: The Ṣalāh, The Ṣalāh!

We are people of ṣalāh. It is core to our identity, as described by the Prophet ﷺ. The masjid is the place of ṣalāh, and its importance is in its direct connection to the ṣalāh.

The caretakers of the masjids need to be people of ṣalāh. We have strangely come across masjid administrators who don't regularly perform ṣalāh or to whom ṣalāh is not a priority. How can a person who doesn't recognize the value of ṣalāh be an administrator of the house of ṣalāh?

The Messenger of Allah ﷺ established ṣalāh as an essential component of our identity. He said, comparing us to people of the other religions, "What distinguishes between us and them is ṣalāh" (Tirmidhi, Nasa'i, Ibn Majah - Sahih).

Ali ibn Abu Talib, may Allah be pleased with him, tells us that one of the last words which the Messenger of Allah ﷺ spoke were: "The ṣalāh, The ṣalāh!" (Abu Dawud – Sahih).

Ṣalāh has a central place in our existence because Allah, the Exalted, commands us:

حَٰفِظُوا عَلَى ٱلصَّلَوَٰتِ

Guard strictly the ṣalāh. (*Qur'an 2: 238*)

Ṣalāh is integral to our success. Allah, the Exalted, gives us this good news:

قَدْ أَفْلَحَ ٱلْمُؤْمِنُونَ

Successful indeed are the believers. (*Qur'an 23:1*)

Our Lord goes on to describe us, the believers, as successful people with many virtues. The very first characteristic He describes about us is our tranquility and focus in ṣalāh:

ٱلَّذِينَ هُمْ فِى صَلَاتِهِمْ خَٰشِعُونَ

They are most humble in their ṣalāh. (*Qur'an 23:2*)

Then the final quality our Lord mentions about the believers is again about the prayer:

وَٱلَّذِينَ هُمْ عَلَىٰ صَلَوَٰتِهِمْ يُحَافِظُونَ

They are very guarded about their ṣalāh. (*Qur'an 23:9*)

When we perform our ṣalāh correctly, it becomes a shield that protects us from immorality and evil. Allah instructs us,

وَأَقِمِ ٱلصَّلَوٰةَ إِنَّ ٱلصَّلَوٰةَ تَنْهَىٰ عَنِ ٱلْفَحْشَآءِ وَٱلْمُنكَرِ

And establish the ṣalāh; indeed the ṣalāh prevents immorality and evil. (*Qur'an 29:45*)

Furthermore, ṣalāh protects us from anxiety. Allah, the Exalted, describes the human beings as created in a state of anxiety.

إِنَّ ٱلْإِنسَـٰنَ خُلِقَ هَلُوعًا... إِلَّا ٱلْمُصَلِّينَ

Indeed humanity was created anxious... except those who pray. (*Qur'an 70:19, 22*)

When reading the first of the two verses, it sounds like all of humanity is doomed. But then Allah, the Exalted, informs us of the exception to this: the people who are grounded by their prayer. The ṣalāh is a vital component to our emotional and spiritual well-being.

The significance of ṣalāh is not only relevant to Islam in its modern form, as it was not a new concept introduced by our Prophet Muhammad ﷺ. Allah the Exalted emphasizes in the Qur'an that all the prophets (peace be upon them) who came from Allah carried a single, unified, and consistent message. Starting from our father Adam (peace be upon him), and then continuing on to over one hundred thousand prophets whose names we may or may not know, all of God's prophets came with the same core message. Allah summarizes all the religions that ever came to earth from Him:

وَمَآ أُمِرُوٓا۟ إِلَّا لِيَعْبُدُوا۟ ٱللَّهَ مُخْلِصِينَ لَهُ ٱلدِّينَ حُنَفَآءَ وَيُقِيمُوا۟ ٱلصَّلَوٰةَ وَيُؤْتُوا۟ ٱلزَّكَوٰةَ وَذَٰلِكَ دِينُ ٱلْقَيِّمَةِ

They were not commanded except to worship Allah alone with sincerity to Him in religion, to establish the ṣalāh, and to pay the zakat, this is the manifest religion (*Qur'an 98:5*)

This ayah teaches us that the religion is based on three things: sincerity, ṣalāh, and zakāh. Muslims thus must first devote all they do to Allah, worship Him individually through the rituals that He revealed, and be good to His creations. These are the essential elements; everything else are details that complete the religion.

This is the status of ṣalāh in Islam. No prophet ever came with any religion that could be acceptable to Allah that did not have ṣalāh in it. All the prophets prayed, although some of the details of their rituals may have differed from our rituals.

The first part of Islam taught to a new Muslim is always ṣalāh. The importance of ṣalāh is such that the very first day Musa (peace be upon him) became a prophet, Allah the Exalted commanded:

إِنَّنِيٓ أَنَا ٱللَّهُ لَآ إِلَٰهَ إِلَّآ أَنَا۠ فَٱعْبُدْنِي وَأَقِمِ ٱلصَّلَوٰةَ لِذِكْرِيٓ

Indeed I am Allah. There is no deity except Me. Therefore worship Me and establish ṣalāh to remember Me. (*Qur'an 20:14*)

Ṣalāh is not a small matter. Allah the Most High sent the noblest of angels to come from the seventh heaven down to the earth to show the Messenger of Allah ﷺ how to perform wuḍūʾ and ṣalāh.

Zayd bin Harithah (may Allah be pleased with him) related from the Prophet ﷺ that Jibreel, may Allah exalt his mention, came to him at the beginning of the revelation and taught him ablution and the prayer. (Ahmad, Ibn Maajah - Ḥasan)

Allah described Jibreel and his relationship to the Qur'an as follows:

إِنَّهُۥ لَقَوْلُ رَسُولٍ كَرِيمٍ ﴿١٩﴾ ذِي قُوَّةٍ عِندَ ذِي ٱلْعَرْشِ مَكِينٍ ﴿٢٠﴾
مُّطَاعٍ ثَمَّ أَمِينٍ ﴿٢١﴾

Indeed this is a word conveyed by a noble messenger, authorized with power by the Owner of the Throne, secure in position, obeyed in the heavens and trustworthy. (*Qur'an 81:19-21*)

Jibreel is the noble carrier of the words of Allah; the one who is endowed with authority by Allah, the Owner of the throne. This honorable angel is the one who came down to demonstrate to the Prophet ﷺ how to perform ṣalāh.

At a crucial point in the life of our leader Muhammad ﷺ, Allah, the Exalted, summoned him from the earth to the heavens for the famous "Night Journey" (*al-Isrāʿ wal-Miʿrāj*). The Prophet ﷺ went past the seventh heaven and past the furthest lote tree (*sidrat al-muntaha*), and then he was honored by permission to approach the throne of Allah the Glorified & Magnificent, where he had a private meeting with Allah. No one else in the history of human existence has ever received such an honor. That conversation was the most important conversation to ever take place, and in it Allah mandated the five daily prayers. This origin story of what we often belittle as a burdensome chore shows us that the matter of ṣalāh is a big deal. We often don't appreciate its tremendous value and role in our relationship with Allah.[1]

The first deed for which Muslims will be taken account of is his or her ṣalāh. Whoever answers this easily will find everything that follows to be easy, but whoever does not will be destroyed. Abu Hurairah narrates that the Messenger of Allah ﷺ said: "Indeed the first deed by which a servant will be called to account on the Day of Resurrection is his ṣalāh. If it is complete, then he is successful and saved, but if it is defective, then he has failed and lost. If something is deficient in his obligatory prayers, then the Lord, Mighty and Sublime, says: 'See if my worshipper has any voluntary prayers.' So then the deficiencies in his obligatory prayers are covered by his voluntary prayers, and the rest of his deeds will be treated like that" (Tirmidhi - Sahih).

The relationship between a Muslim and the ṣalāh is awe inspiring. Many people of other faiths have remarked upon the tranquility, awe, and holiness they feel when they observe Muslims in ṣalāh. People have envied our deep personal relationship with the Creator of the heavens and the earth. Some have even entered Islam because of ṣalāh.

One brother recounts that he became Muslim after witnessing ṣalāh for the first time. He saw the people line up as equal servants to the One God and he realized that Islam was the correct religion—the religion designed by his Creator for him.

Another brother described how both a pastor and an imam came to preach their religions in his animist, spirit worshipping village in Ethiopia. The pastor invited him to pray once a week, and the imam invited him to pray five times a day. He reasoned that if prayer were to be a good thing for people, then more prayer would bring more goodness to him. This elementary yet flawless logic led him to choose the message of Islam.

Ṣalāh is not a duty; it is a gift. It is an opportunity to communicate directly with Allah. It is a private audience with the King of kings. Speaking to

1 This hadith is narrated by Anas bin Malik in *Sahih al-Bukhari.* It says in part: Musa said, "O Lord! I thought that none would be raised up above me." But Gabriel ascended with him (the Prophet) for a distance above that, the distance of which only Allah knows, till he reached the furthest Lote Tree and then the Irresistible, the Lord of Honor and Majesty approached and came closer till he (Gabriel) was about two bow lengths or nearer. Among the things that Allah revealed to him then, was: "Fifty prayers were enjoined on his followers in a day and a night." (Please see: https://sunnah.com/bukhari/97/142 See also: Fath Al-Bari Page 263, 264, Vol. 17)

the Giver of life and death, the One who rewards with Paradise and punishes with Hell is no small thing! Allah the Exalted says in the Qur'an:

حَـٰفِظُوا عَلَى ٱلصَّلَوَٰتِ وَٱلصَّلَوٰةِ ٱلْوُسْطَىٰ

Guard strictly your prayers, especially the middle prayer. (*Qur'an 2:238*)

The middle prayer described here is ʿAṣr. Abdullah ibn Umar (may Allah be pleased with him) narrated that the Messenger of Allah ﷺ said, "Whoever missed the Asr prayer, it is as if he was robbed of his family and his property" (Tirmidhi - Ṣaḥeeḥ).

The middle prayer has this importance because it interrupts our work cycle before the day finishes, when we usually have that temptation of allowing our worldly concerns to interrupt our connection to our Lord. The wisdom of five daily prayers is for the Muslim to remember Allah at all times.

We often fail to appreciate the reality of our human condition. We are not only material creatures, but also spiritual creatures. Just as the human body will wither and decay unless fed three times a day, the human soul also needs its routine of nutrition. If it is not nourished, the human soul will decline and deteriorate.

The components of the ṣalāh, such as standing (*qiyām*), kneeling (*julūs*), bowing (*rukūʾ*) and prostration (*sujūd*) all existed in the prayers of the followers of prophets before us. However, some things have changed over time by Allah's command. This is because ṣalāh is exclusively for Allah, and He only accepts it in the manner He has outlined. The people before us performed ṣalāh as their prophets (peace be upon them) taught them, and so we perform ṣalāh as our prophet Muhammad ﷺ taught us. All other methods are prohibited and unacceptable.

In the Qur'an, Allah describes Zakaria (peace be upon him) engaged in the standing (*qiyām*) portion of ṣalāh:

وَهُوَ قَآئِمٌ يُصَلِّى فِى ٱلْمِحْرَابِ

... while he was standing in prayer in his chamber. (*Qur'an 3:39*)

Allah commanded Mariam (peace be upon her) to perform *sujūd* and *rukūʿ*:

يَـٰمَرْيَمُ ٱقْنُتِى لِرَبِّكِ وَٱسْجُدِى وَٱرْكَعِى مَعَ ٱلرَّٰكِعِينَ

O Mary! Be devout to your Lord, prostrate yourself in prayer and bow along with those who bow down. (*Qur'an 3:43*)

The following Bible citations even show that the previous prophets performed ablution (*wuḍūʿ*), bowing (*rukūʾ*), and prostration (*sujūd*):

> "And Moses and Aaron and his sons washed their hands and their feet thereat; When they went into the tent of the congregation, and when they came near unto the altar, they washed; as the Lord commanded Moses." [Exodus 40:31-32]
>
> "O come, let us worship and bow down: let us kneel before the Lord our maker." [Psalm 95:6]
>
> "And Joshua fell on his face to the earth, and did worship" [Joshua 5:14]
>
> "And Abraham fell on his face: and God talked with him" [Genesis 17:3]

There are some things that have changed over time by the command of Allah. We provide three examples:

Aisha (may Allah be pleased with her) narrates that the Messenger of Allah ﷺ said, "Every prayer in which the Mother of the Book is not recited is deficient." (Ibn Majah – Hassan). The mother of the book is Sura al-Fatiha. Given that the nations before us did not have Sura al Fatiha, they must have established ṣalāh without Fatiha, but this change has been mandated for us.

Also, the concept of ṣalāh wasn't first commanded in the aforementioned scene of the Night Journey. It was practiced at the very beginning of the prophethood of Muhammad ﷺ, but was performed twice a day. During the Night Journey the number of daily prayers was changed to five.

Another example of a changed feature of ṣalāh for the Muslims is the direction of prayer. At the beginning the Muslims prayed facing Jerusalem like the followers of earlier Prophets, but then Allah, the Exalted, commanded the Muslims to start praying facing the Kaaba in Mecca. This drew some criticism from the people of the book in Medina at the time, but was nothing more than a test to see who would worship according to their own whims, and who would worship God according to His terms.

The importance of ṣalāh is so great that we are commanded to pray even if we are in fear of our life. Allah the Exalted commands,

فَإِنْ خِفْتُمْ فَرِجَالًا أَوْ رُكْبَانًا

And if you fear an enemy then perform ṣalāh on foot or while mounted. (*Qur'an 2:239*)

Allah, our Lord, further commands us to resume normal ṣalāh after the immediate threat of the battle is over:

فَإِذَآ أَمِنتُمْ فَٱذْكُرُوا ٱللَّهَ كَمَا عَلَّمَكُم مَّا لَمْ تَكُونُوا تَعْلَمُونَ

But when you are secure, then remember Allah [in prayer], as He has taught you that which you did not previously know. (Qur'an 2:239)

Emphasizing the importance of praying on time, Allah, the Exalted, says,

إِنَّ ٱلصَّلَوٰةَ كَانَتْ عَلَى ٱلْمُؤْمِنِينَ كِتَٰبًا مَّوْقُوتًا

Indeed the prayer has been commanded upon the believers at appointed times. (Qur'an 4:103)

These appointed times are meant to nurture our souls, to bring unity to the ummah, to instil in us obedience to our Lord, and to provide an oasis of spirituality in our daily lives. This is why the Prophet ﷺ said,"The best of deeds in the sight of Allah is ṣalāh at the beginning of its time" (Bukhari).

The masjid is a living monument to ṣalāh. We are the ummah of ṣalāh. It fuels us, it defines us, and it governs our daily schedule.

Chapter 2: The Houses of Allah

It is a great mercy from Allah, the Exalted, that He has permitted houses to be built that belong to Him, wherein He permits His name to be glorified. Allah the Exalted says,

فِي بُيُوتٍ أَذِنَ ٱللَّهُ أَن تُرْفَعَ وَيُذْكَرَ فِيهَا ٱسْمُهُۥ يُسَبِّحُ لَهُۥ فِيهَا بِٱلْغُدُوِّ وَٱلْآصَالِ

... in houses that Allah has permitted to be built where His name shall be mentioned; exalting in the morning and the evenings. (Qur'an 24:36)

Abu Huraira (may Allah be pleased with him) reported that the Messenger of Allah ﷺ said, "The parts of earth dearest to Allah are its masjids" (Muslim – Sahih). Our Lord the Most Glorious loves the masjids so much that He has claimed all of them exclusively for Himself.

وَأَنَّ ٱلْمَسَٰجِدَ لِلَّهِ فَلَا تَدْعُوا مَعَ ٱللَّهِ أَحَدًا

And indeed, the masjids are for Allah, so do not invoke anyone else with Allah. (Qur'an 72:18)

There are houses that Allah has claimed for Himself, and Allah has honored the masjid by calling it His house. These houses have a certain dignity that must be maintained. Those who sit in the first row get more reward than those who sit in the second. The higher honor comes to the person who comes early enough to sit in the first row, and the rule in general in a masjid is that whoever comes should sit as far to the front as possible without climbing over other people's shoulders. The Messenger of Allah ﷺ said, "If they knew what [goodness] there is in the first row, they would cast lots for it" (Ibn Majah – Ṣaḥīḥ).

The Messenger of Allah ﷺ also said: "The best rows for men are the first rows, and the worst ones are the last ones. The best rows for women are the last ones and the worst ones for them are the first ones" (Muslim – Sahih). Please note that many scholars hold this to apply only when there is no partition or wall between the rows for men and women.

A man entered the mosque one Friday when the Messenger of Allah ﷺ was delivering the sermon. He started stepping over the people's shoulders to come forward, and so the Messenger of Allah ﷺ said: "Sit down, for you have annoyed people, and you are late" (Ibn Majah – Ṣaḥīḥ).

We should sit quietly in the masjid, not distracting others. It is permissible to talk about anything, but we must understand that there are people in the masjid who are engaged in worship, and so the dignity of the masjid should be maintained by showing respect and courtesy to them.

Sometimes we take this too far, leaving no room for children in the house of Allah. Even though the *adab* of the Masjid is serious, we must accept that children will do childish things in the masjid. This will help normalize their presence and help them feel comfortable and excited to come to the masjid.

The Messenger of Allah ﷺ said, "The angels invoke blessings upon any of you for as long as he is in the place where he prayed, and as long as he does not invalidate his ablution, they say: 'O Allah, forgive him, O Allah, have mercy on him" (Nasa'i - Ṣaḥeeḥ). So if you are not busy, stay after the ṣalāh, sit down, and relax. Remember Allah, contemplate His majesty and perfection, or read the Qur'an.

The ṣalāh is supposed to be a dignified event. For example, we have been instructed to not run toward ṣalāh when the Imam has already started, because the masjid is not supposed to have undignified running inside it. The Messenger of Allah ﷺ prohibited this, specifically mentioning dignity, when he said, "When you come to pray, do not come rushing; come walking in a dignified manner, and whatever you catch up with, pray; and whatever you miss, make it up" (Nasa'i - Ṣaḥeeḥ).

There is even a proper protocol of entering a masjid, exiting it, sitting in it, staying in it and praying in it. The Messenger of Allah ﷺ taught us the special dua to say when we enter: "O Allah, open for me the gates of your mercy" (Nasa'i – Sahih).

He also teaches us that on the way out, we should say, "O Allah, I ask you for your bounty" (Nasa'i – Sahih).

In another authentic Hadith, the Messenger of Allah ﷺ taught us to pray a voluntary prayer as a way of greeting the mosque (تحيّة المسجد). He said, "When any one of you enters the masjid, let him pray two rakahs before he sits down" (Nasa'i – Sahih). Out of respect for the dignity of the masjid, we should not sit down after entering the masjid without praying two rakʿahs. This is the Sunnah.

There is a disagreement about what to do if we enter while the Jumuʿah khutba is going on. In the Shafiʿi and Hanbali schools, a Muslim should still pray the prayer of greeting the mosque, but make it short and fast. In the Hanafi and Maliki schools, listening to the khutba is mandatory and the prayer of greeting the mosque is recommended, so it is better to sit and listen to the khutba.[1]

In another Hadith, the Messenger of Allah ﷺ said: "Whoever is in the masjid waiting for the prayer is in a state of prayer" (Nasa'i - Hasan). So the mere act of waiting in the masjid for the prayer to start gives us the reward of being in prayer for the duration of that time.

The Messenger of Allah ﷺ taught us that, "Whoever does wudu' properly, then walks to the prescribed prayer, and prays with the people or with the congregation or in the masjid, Allah will forgive him for his sins." (Nasa'i - Sahih)

The Messenger of Allah ﷺ also said, "Prayer performed by a man in congregation is rewarded twenty five degrees more than a prayer performed alone in his house or in the market. This is because when any of you performs ablution and does it perfectly, and goes out to the mosque having no intention but to pray, and nothing moving him except for the prayer, then with every step he takes, his rank is elevated by one degree and one sin is remitted from him until he enters the masjid. When he enters the masjid, he will be counted as praying for as long as he is waiting for the prayer. The angels continue to invoke blessings on any of you so long as he remains seated in the place he prayed; they say: 'O Allah, forgive him! O Allah, have mercy on him! O Allah, accept his repentance so long as he does not harm anyone, or breaks his ablution!'" (Abu Dawud - Sahih).

Congratulating those who go to the masjid for the Isha and Fajr prayers, the Messenger of Allah ﷺ said, "Give good news to those who walk to the mosque in the darkness, for they will be given full light on the day of Resurrection." (Abu Dawud - Sahih).

To leave the masjid without praying in congregation after the adhan has been called is a violation of the masjid's dignity. Abu al-Shatha said, "We were sitting with Abu Hurairah in the masjid when a man left the masjid after the adhan for the afternoon prayer had been called. Abu Hurairah said, 'This man has disobeyed Abu al-Qasim," referring to the Prophet ﷺ (Abu Dawud - Sahih).

The Masjid of our Prophet ﷺ was always clean. The companions loved the masjid and took care of it. The Messenger of Allah ﷺ even deemed spitting inside of the masjid to be sinful (Bukhari, Muslim). Anas (may Allah be pleased with him) narrates that the Prophet ﷺ saw some mucus in the front of the masjid and he became so angry that his face turned red. Then a

1 Awqāf Kuwait" .Ṣalāt al-Jumuʿah "*Al-Mawsūʿah al-Fiqhiyyah* ,1983 ,p.205 .

woman from the Ansar came and scraped it off, and put some perfume on it. The Messenger of Allah ﷺ praised her action (Ibn Majah, Nasa'i – Sahih).

My teacher once told me that when he was young, straightening the shoes was one of the tasks assigned to children like him as they entered the masjid. This taught him at an early age the importance of serving the masjid and the importance of cleanness and neatness. This used to be the norm in masjids, but nowadays we often enter the masjid and fail to take any action to make the space neat and clean. Nobody feels the need to pick up any scraps of trash that they might see and throw it away.

The congregants of a masjid should physically labor for it, by sweeping the floor, vacuuming the carpets, cleaning the bathroom and cleaning the parking lot. This is a way of maintaining the masjid. Even people far away from the masjid should help by donating money to sustain it.

Chapter 3: The Noble Guardians

The masjid is the beating heart of the Muslim society. The contribution to constructing, supervising, and managing the masjid is a critical role for a Muslim. Only people who are very fortunate are allowed by Allah the honor and the dignity of being a masjid caretaker.

Allah, the Exalted, tells us:

إِنَّمَا يَعْمُرُ مَسَٰجِدَ ٱللَّهِ مَنْ ءَامَنَ بِٱللَّهِ وَٱلْيَوْمِ ٱلْءَاخِرِ وَأَقَامَ ٱلصَّلَوٰةَ وَءَاتَى ٱلزَّكَوٰةَ وَلَمْ يَخْشَ إِلَّا ٱللَّهَ فَعَسَىٰٓ أُولَٰٓئِكَ أَن يَكُونُوا مِنَ ٱلْمُهْتَدِينَ

"The masjids of Allah shall be visited and maintained by such as believe in Allah and the last day, establish regular prayers, and pay charity, and fear none at all except Allah. It is they who are expected to be on true guidance." (Qur'an 9:18)

Allah the Exalted describes the special class of people who have been given authority or permission by Allah to serve His houses. For a person to be a caretaker, a regular visitor, or a custodian of the masjid, the person must have the following qualifications:

1. Belief in Allah

Not everybody can be a caretaker of a masjid. Those who are so intricately involved in maintaining Allah's house must believe in Allah as their Lord and Creator. People who are unduly skeptical of religion and not mindful of God cannot properly understand the purpose and needs of a masjid, regardless of their technical or administrative skills. We certainly do need architects, structural engineers, and contractors to build it, and we need accountants, lawyers and facility managers to operate it, but without belief in Allah, this is merely a professional exercise devoid of any spiritual purpose. In fact, the masjid caretaker has to maintain a close personal relationship with Allah, whose house they are custodians of.

2. Belief in the last day

The caretaker of a masjid must clearly understand that he or she is going to die. They will one day stand in front of the Owner of this masjid. Without this sense of accountability, their efforts can be detrimental to the masjid and its community.

3. Establishing regular prayers

Allah the Exalted mentioned the importance of prayer numerous times in the Qur'an. The wording used, to "establish the prayer, alludes to the fact that it is about more than just the movements and words., iIt means to make arrangements for the prayer, to uphold it and normalize it, such that one becomes a person of ṣalāh and wants to pray wherever he goes.

Allah the Exalted explained this concept in another ayah. He describes the good people:

ٱلَّذِينَ إِن مَّكَّنَّٰهُمْ فِى ٱلْأَرْضِ أَقَامُوا۟ ٱلصَّلَوٰةَ

"Those who, if We give them authority in the land, establish ṣalāh." (*Qur'an 22:41*)

The first job of a Sultan or ruler is to establish the prayer. If Allah gives a Muslim authority over a house (when he buys it or rents it), then his first duty is to establish the prayer in that house.

The Messenger of Allah ﷺ described the house in which prayer is not established as a graveyard. Imam Muslim (may Allah have mercy on him) placed only one hadith in the chapter of Sahih Muslim entitled, "It is recommended to offer voluntary prayers in one's house". Abu Huraira (may Allah be pleased with him) reported Allah's Messenger ﷺ as saying, "Do not make your houses as graveyards. Satan runs away from the house in which Surah Baqara is recited" (Muslim – Sahih).

All Muslims should understand that establishing the prayer is a mandate from Allah. Establish the prayer means to uphold it and perform it under all conditions. Included within the task of establishing the ṣalāh is to (i) construct the masjid, (ii) make the masjid easily accessible, and (iii) hire an imam. A person who doesn't understand the divine mandate of establishing prayer cannot be a caretaker of a masjid.

4. Paying charity

It's not enough for this person to contribute time and efforts. He must contribute from his wealth as well. Allah says,

وَٱلَّذِينَ فِىٓ أَمْوَٰلِهِمْ حَقٌّ مَّعْلُومٌ

"And those in whose wealth is a recognized right." (*Qur'an 70:24*)

The houses of Allah are built with the *sadaqa* (charity) of the servants of Allah. A person who does not practice this cannot urge and convince his fellow Muslims to sacrifice financially for the masjid.

5. Fearing only Allah

This is an important requirement especially in the West where masjids are under the constant threat of Islamophobia. The caretakers of a masjid should fear none except Allah. Allah the Exalted has a deal for those who embody this:

فَعَسَىٰٓ أُولَـٰٓئِكَ أَن يَكُونُوا۟ مِنَ ٱلْمُهْتَدِينَ

"It is hoped that these are the ones who are expected to be the guided ones." (*Qur'an 9:18*)

Other Criteria

In addition to the qualifications listed above, the guardians of a house of Allah need to possess management skills, customer relations skills, financial skills, and organizational skills.

Rewards of the Guardians of the Masjid

The Messenger of Allah ﷺ migrated from Mecca to Medina, primarily because the Islamophobia in Mecca prevented him from worshiping his Lord. Abdullah bin Adiy bin Hamra (may Allah be pleased with him) said, "I saw the Messenger of Allah ﷺ, when he was on his camel, standing in Al-Hazwarah (in Mecca) saying, 'By Allah, you are the best land of Allah, and the dearest of the land of Allah to me. By Allah, had I not been expelled from you I would never have left'" (Ibn Majah – Sahih).

The people of Quraysh pursued him. They had a bounty of a hundred camels on his head to bring him back dead or alive. The Messenger of Allah ﷺ traveled at night and hid in a cave, and eventually he came to the city of Yathrib (which was renamed Medina). He came first to the borders of Yathrib to a place called Quba. He was tired and exhausted, so he and Abu Bakr (may Allah be pleased with him) decided to rest for a few days in Quba. Most scholars agree he stayed there for four days.[1]

In that brief period, the Messenger of Allah ﷺ built the masjid of Quba, leaving a sign in Quba of his presence there. It was the importance of establishing the ṣalāh that drove him to build a masjid in Quba.

1 Saifur Rahman al-Mubarakpuri *Ar Raheeq Al Makhtum The Sealed Nectar* .Darussalam Publications2002 .
Please see: http://kalamullah.com/Books/Ar-Raheeq%20Al-Makhtum.pdf

What will we say when we meet Prophet Muhammad ﷺ on the Day of Judgment, and he asks us what city we used to live in? And then if he asks us if we built a masjid there? Did we establish the ṣalāh? We all have a duty: if we're in a place without a masjid, then we have to build it. If a masjid exists, then we have to maintain it.

This responsibility, in reality, is an opportunity. Allah the Exalted confers dignity and guidance upon whoever builds and maintains His house. The Messenger of Allah ﷺ said: "whoever builds for Allah a masjid, Allah will reward him similar to it in paradise." (Bukhari & Muslim - Sahih)

This reward is not only available for rich people, Allah will reward us even for a small donation. In another narration, the Messenger of Allah ﷺ said: "Whosoever shares in building a masjid for Allah, even if it is as small as a bird's nest, Allah will build for him a house in Paradise" (Ahmad - Sahih).

Allah the Exalted asks us a question:

مَّن ذَا ٱلَّذِى يُقْرِضُ ٱللَّهَ قَرْضًا حَسَنًا فَيُضَٰعِفَهُۥ لَهُۥٓ أَضْعَافًا كَثِيرَةً وَٱللَّهُ يَقْبِضُ وَيَبْصُۜطُ وَإِلَيْهِ تُرْجَعُونَ

"Who will lend to Allah a beautiful loan, which Allah will double and multiply many times? It is Allah that gives restriction or plenty, and to Him shall be your return." (*Qur'an 2:245*)

Allah the Exalted makes a promise about this loan. He promises a rate of return of at least one hundred percent. He might double it, or He might multiply it many times over.

In Surah *Muhammad*, Allah the Exalted sheds light on the consequence of refusing to give for His sake:

هَٰٓأَنتُمْ هَٰٓؤُلَآءِ تُدْعَوْنَ لِتُنفِقُوا۟ فِى سَبِيلِ ٱللَّهِ فَمِنكُم مَّن يَبْخَلُ وَمَن يَبْخَلْ فَإِنَّمَا يَبْخَلُ عَن نَّفْسِهِۦ وَٱللَّهُ ٱلْغَنِىُّ وَأَنتُمُ ٱلْفُقَرَآءُ وَإِن تَتَوَلَّوْا۟ يَسْتَبْدِلْ قَوْمًا غَيْرَكُمْ ثُمَّ لَا يَكُونُوٓا۟ أَمْثَٰلَكُم

"Here you are—you are being called to spend in the path of Allah, and among you are some who are stingy. Whoever is stingy, is only stingy towards his own soul. And Allah is rich, while you are the ones in need . And if you still turn away, He will replace you with a different people, and they will not be like you." (*Qur'an 47:38*)

Allah, the Exalted, owns all the wealth imaginable. He doesn't need our money. He instructs us to give our money because it's good for us, and He wants us to benefit ourselves by this act of charity.

In the verse above, Allah issues a solemn promise. Allah will cause His religion to survive, either at our hands or at the hands of a different people, if we don't do our job. Although it is the duty of each Muslim to stand up and advocate for Islam, Allah the Exalted forbids us to think even for a moment that He has no alternative means of carrying out His victory besides us.

Many communities before us didn't listen to this warning, so Allah replaced them. He brought forth people who were better than them, and the new people were not stingy and greedy like the people before them. This happened even in this Ummah, if we consider the situation of Al-Quds, the crusaders were only given victory there after the Muslims began to fall short in their responsibilities. It remained like this for almost one hundred years until the Muslims learned their lesson and chose to follow the Qur'an. Then Allah, the Exalted, gave them victory, and these people were more grateful and dutiful than their predecessors. We can see the same pattern in the failures and successes of Muslim communities all across the world and over centuries.

If a group of Muslims disobeys the commands of Allah, then they should not be surprised when Allah tests them with weakness and defeat. We must understand that Allah promised to protect His religion, and He has promised to defend and assist those who carry His religion. He didn't promise to defend and assist all Muslims.

The verse above is terrifying, but at the same time thought provoking. It explains the dynamic nature of the relationship between Allah and this Ummah. Allah, the Exalted, makes clear to us that there is a particular type of behavior He is looking for from people. If we demonstrate this behavior, it's good for us, if we do not, another group will arise and carry out this task.

Chapter 4: al-Masjid al-Nabawi, the Ideal Masjid

Allah the Exalted describes himself in Surat An-Nur in order for us to understand how to relate to Him:

ٱللَّهُ نُورُ ٱلسَّمَٰوَٰتِ وَٱلْأَرْضِ مَثَلُ نُورِهِۦ كَمِشْكَوٰةٍ فِيهَا مِصْبَاحٌ ٱلْمِصْبَاحُ فِى زُجَاجَةٍ ٱلزُّجَاجَةُ كَأَنَّهَا كَوْكَبٌ دُرِّىٌّ يُوقَدُ مِن شَجَرَةٍ مُّبَٰرَكَةٍ زَيْتُونَةٍ لَّا شَرْقِيَّةٍ وَلَا غَرْبِيَّةٍ يَكَادُ زَيْتُهَا يُضِىٓءُ وَلَوْ لَمْ تَمْسَسْهُ نَارٌ نُّورٌ عَلَىٰ نُورٍ يَهْدِى ٱللَّهُ لِنُورِهِۦ مَن يَشَآءُ وَيَضْرِبُ ٱللَّهُ ٱلْأَمْثَٰلَ لِلنَّاسِ وَٱللَّهُ بِكُلِّ شَىْءٍ عَلِيمٌ

"Allah is the Light of the heavens and the earth. The example of His light is like a niche within which is a lamp; the lamp is within glass, and the glass is as if it were a pearly [white] star lit from [the oil of] a blessed olive tree, neither of the east nor of the west, whose oil would almost glow even if untouched by fire. Light upon light! Allah guides to His light whom He wills. Allah presents examples for the people, and Allah is Knowing of all things." (Qur'an 24:35)

This ayah is among the ambiguous verses (*mutashabihat*). We do not understand these literally, but they are meant to help us get a spiritual or emotional connection to things that our brains cannot understand properly. The human intellect cannot fully and properly understand Allah. In His infinite mercy, He provides us emotional and spiritual ways by which we can understand with our hearts so that we may know how to interact with Him.

In the next verse, Allah tells us this lamp is to be found in houses that Allah has given permission to be built.

فِى بُيُوتٍ أَذِنَ ٱللَّهُ أَن تُرْفَعَ وَيُذْكَرَ فِيهَا ٱسْمُهُۥ يُسَبِّحُ لَهُۥ فِيهَا بِٱلْغُدُوِّ وَٱلْءَاصَالِ

In houses which Allah has ordered to be raised and that His name be mentioned therein; exalting Him within them in the morning and the evenings. (Qur'an 24:36)

These houses have a special connection to Allah. This ayah is not only referring to the Kaaba or al-Masjid al-Nabawi. It is about *all* of Allah's houses. This verse describes all the houses of Allah that He has permitted to be raised.

If we want to know what the ideal masjid is, then we must turn to the Messenger of Allah ﷺ. Allah says:

لَّقَدْ كَانَ لَكُمْ فِي رَسُولِ ٱللَّهِ أُسْوَةٌ حَسَنَةٌ

Indeed for you in the Messenger of Allah is the ideal example to follow. (Qur'an 33:21)

Allah sent His Messenger with the job of teaching us Islam, and doing so entailed establishing the perfect masjid and demonstrating to people how to operate it.

Sometimes people think of a real masjid as a building with minarets and domes and various other decorative features, but that is not part of the characteristics of an ideal masjid. The Messenger of Allah ﷺ never built a minaret or a dome. These features are nice to have, but are absolutely not essential.

The original Masjid of the Prophet ﷺ was a very simple structure. The floor was sand that would turn to sticky sludge in the rain, the roof made of leaves from a date palm stood on palm-trunk pillars, and the walls were made of bricks of dried mud.

Abdullah bin Umar (may Allah be pleased with him) described it in exactly these terms, as he reported, "The masjid (of the Prophet) during his lifetime was built with bricks, its roof with branches of the palm-tree, and its pillars with palm-wood. Mujahid, a later scholar, said that Abu Bakr (may Allah be pleased with him) did not add anything to it, but Umar (may Allah be pleased with him) added to it. He reconstructed it as it was during the lifetime of the Messenger of Allah ﷺ with bricks and branches, but he changed its pillars. Uthman (may Allah be pleased with him) then changed it altogether with increasing additions. He built its walls with decorated stone and lime. And he built the pillars with decorated stone and its roof with teak.[1]

Abu Saeed Al-Khudri (may Allah be pleased with him) narrates, "A cloud came and it rained until the roof started leaking, and in those days the roof used to be of the branches of date-palms. The call to prayer was pronounced,

1 This is a Sahih report by Abu Dawud.

and I saw Allah's Messenger ﷺ prostrating in water and mud. I saw the mark of mud on his forehead" (Bukhari – Sahih).

The perfect masjid is not about the building. It's about what happens inside the building. The characteristics of the masjid that the Messenger of Allah ﷺ established are as follows:

1. The masjid should be dedicated to the worship of Allah.
2. The masjid should be a center for teaching Islam.
3. The masjid should be a center for all knowledge, including the secular sciences.
4. The masjid should be welcoming to everyone including children, youth, women and new Muslims.
5. The masjid should be the center of the Muslim community.
6. The masjid should be a center for *daʿwah*.
7. The masjid should provide social services.

We have already discussed the masjid as a place of ṣalāh in the beginning of this book. In the following chapter, *in shāʾ Allah,* we shall cover the rest of these aspects.

Chapter 5: Radiating Knowledge

The very first word revealed in the Qur'an was the word "read" (*iqra*). The revelation of this first word of the Qur'an affirmed the status of our beloved Prophet Muhammad ﷺ as the final messenger, and it brought us, his followers, the Ummah of Muhammad ﷺ into existence. Thus, our religion and our entire civilization is based upon knowledge.

ٱقْرَأْ بِٱسْمِ رَبِّكَ ٱلَّذِى خَلَقَ

Read in the name of your Lord, Who created. (*Qur'an 96:1*)

Many scholars have discussed the significance of our Lord, the Most High, choosing the word "read" as His very first communication to humanity. Since that initial proclamation, acquiring and spreading knowledge became a major endeavor of the entire Muslim community. Allah, the Exalted, commanded us to seek knowledge and to continuously ask Allah to increase our knowledge.

وَقُل رَّبِّ زِدْنِى عِلْمًا

And say, "My Lord! Increase me in knowledge." (*Qur'an 20:114*)

Anas bin Malik (may Allah be pleased with him) narrates that the Prophet Muhammad ﷺ declared, "Acquiring knowledge is obligatory upon every Muslim" (Ibn Majah, Tirmidhi - Sahih).

The acquisition of knowledge is not just a requirement upon us; we benefit ourselves from it greatly. For example, our Lord, the Most Generous has promised to honor and elevate us through knowledge:

يَرْفَعِ ٱللَّهُ ٱلَّذِينَ ءَامَنُوا مِنكُمْ وَٱلَّذِينَ أُوتُوا ٱلْعِلْمَ دَرَجَٰتٍ

Allah will exalt those of you who believe and have been given knowledge to high ranks. (*Qur'an 58:11*)

Then after commanding us to acquire knowledge and promising to honor us through it, the Most Merciful teaches us that knowledge is one of the best types of wealth we can possess:

يُؤْتِى ٱلْحِكْمَةَ مَن يَشَآءُ وَمَن يُؤْتَ ٱلْحِكْمَةَ فَقَدْ أُوتِىَ خَيْرًا كَثِيرًا وَمَا يَذَّكَّرُ إِلَّآ أُولُوا ٱلْأَلْبَٰبِ

He gives wisdom to whomever He wills. And whoever is given wisdom is given abundant wealth. And none will be mindful but those of reason. (*Qur'an 2:269*)

It is not surprising then that the first generation of Muslims made the acquisition of knowledge a major priority for the community. Early Arabia experienced a curious phenomenon. The ability to read and write began to be valued over gold and silver, or their precious livestock. The idea of knowledge as a commodity was made mainstream by the earliest Muslims.

After the battle of Badr, for example, a modification to the traditional customs of war was introduced. When taking ransom for freeing prisoners of war, literate prisoners were permitted to purchase their release simply by teaching ten children to read and write. One Companion recounts,

> Another form of ransom assumed an educational dimension; most of the Makkans, unlike the Madinese, were literate, and so each prisoner who could not afford the ransom was entrusted with ten children to teach them the art of writing and reading. Once the child had been proficient enough, the instructor would be set free.[1]

Furthermore, we know Prophet Muhammad ﷺ approved of a marriage in which the dowry consisted of the teaching and transfer of knowledge. Through these practical examples, the noble companions established among themselves, as well as to the broader society, the idea of knowledge as a valuable commodity.

After the death of our beloved Prophet Muhammad ﷺ, the Muslim ummah unleashed a burst of research, analysis, learning, and dissemination. They invented completely new disciplines of learning, both in the religious and the secular sciences. Of the religious sciences, the Muslim scholars developed the sciences of *tajweed, tafseer,* other sciences of the Qur'an, *mustalah al-hadith* and the studies related to narrator and transmission analysis, fiqh and its underlying principles, seerah, and many others. Within the Arabic language, they compiled the first dictionaries, developed grammar studies, advanced the analysis of literature, excelled at calligraphy, and took poetry to new heights. Muslims made major contributions in the secular sciences as well, including medicine, pharmacology, anatomy, physics, chemistry, geog-

1 Saifur Rahman al-Mubarakpuri. *Ar Raheeq Al Makhtum* The Sealed Nectar. Darussalam Publications. 2002

raphy, astronomy, math, algebra, geometry, trigonometry, accounting, economics, anthropology, and sociology. Muslim inventors shaped the modern world we live in. In fact many words such as average, algebra, algorithm, and cipher, to name just a few, are derivatives of Arabic words.

The earliest Muslims made no distinction between the religious and the secular sciences. This is because our Creator commanded us to examine and ponder upon His creation.

إِنَّ فِي خَلْقِ ٱلسَّمَٰوَٰتِ وَٱلْأَرْضِ وَٱخْتِلَٰفِ ٱلَّيْلِ وَٱلنَّهَارِ لَءَايَٰتٍ لِّأُولِى ٱلْأَلْبَٰبِ

Indeed, in the creation of the heavens and the earth and the alternation of the night and the day are signs for people of understanding. (*Qur'an 3:190*)

Naturally, to the early Muslims, this quest for knowledge, commanded by Allah, began in the house of Allah—the masjid. The first university on earth was built in Qairawan (present day Morocco) by a Muslim woman named Fatima al-Fihri (may Allah increase her reward). This university grew out of a masjid.

We can even see the Arabic influence on the academic world through the terminology of our higher education system. It was customary for a teacher to sit at a pillar of the masjid after ṣalāh to teach. Over time, the word "pillar" (*'amīd*) began to refer to the dean of the department of a particular subject. The english word "college" comes from the Arabic word *kulliyah,* which was the aggregation of multiple fields within a broad area of knowledge. The collection of multiple colleges is called a *jāmiʿah.* The English word university came from this concept; it is universal and gathers all knowledge. All this started out of the masjid.

Even today, in universities across the world, graduates and professors emulate Muslim attire by wearing graduation gowns. Modern graduation gowns have different colors and patterns to distinguish between students, professors, and heads of departments. This is a continuation of the tradition in universities in Andalusia (Muslim Spain), where each student and teacher were issued a free gown that complied with their dress code of different colors and patterns for teachers and students.

One of the main drivers of the growth and dynamism of the Muslim civilization was the constant pursuit and cultivation of knowledge. The Muslim civilization continued thriving until their society became distracted and relaxed in their quest of knowledge. This led to decay and loss, and ultimately to colonization and destruction. One hundred years after the supposed end of colonization, the Muslim civilization is nowhere near where we need to be. We make up almost a quarter of the world population, but we produce far less than a quarter of the PhD degrees granted, patents issued, research papers written, books published, universities established. We have a lot of catching up to do. Our masjids need to reclaim their central role in the pursuit of knowledge.

Among the sciences taught at the masjid should be the sciences of religion. There should be classes available to all ages for the main topics of Qur'an, hadith, *fiqh* and *sīrah*. This is what the Companions and the righteous Caliphs (may Allah be pleased with them) did. The ideal masjid is engaged in religious sciences, while promoting its congregants to pursue all sciences. The masjid should be the center and launchpad for learning.

Chapter 6: The Welcoming Masjid

Our masjids should be welcoming to the entire community, catering to the needs of both men and women. It must be a safe haven for those who are able, handicapped, rich, poor, immigrant and native. The ideal masjid accommodates for the elderly, the working adults, the home makers, and the students, while being supportive and patient with our youth and children. It is the space where people of every nationality and race can feel at home.

Our Lord, the Glorified and Exalted commanded our beloved Messenger ﷺ to be gentle with the people:

فَبِمَا رَحْمَةٍ مِّنَ ٱللَّهِ لِنتَ لَهُمْ وَلَوْ كُنتَ فَظًّا غَلِيظَ ٱلْقَلْبِ
لَٱنفَضُّوا مِنْ حَوْلِكَ

It was by the mercy of Allah that you dealt with them gently. And had you been severe and harsh-hearted, they would have dispersed away from you. (*Qur'an 3:159*)

When we study the life of the noble Messenger of Allah ﷺ, we find that he demonstrated a gentle attitude towards everyone around him. Consequently the al-Masjid al-Nabawi was a very welcoming place. In this chapter we shall discuss four categories of people to whom we must extend the warmest welcome.

Youth Friendly Masjid

The Messenger of Allah ﷺ said: "Whoever does not show mercy to our young, respect our elders, command good, and forbid evil is not one of us" (Tirmidhi – Sahih). With this hadith in mind, it is perplexing to see a masjid where children are not allowed. Who will take the places of the adults in the mosque after they pass away? Do we want our masjids to become empty museums? How will the empty building serve the purpose of worshipping Allah?

The Prophet ﷺ also said, "When I stand for prayer, I intend to prolong it. But upon hearing the cries of a child, I cut it short, as I dislike to trouble the child's mother" (Bukhari).

Abdullah bin Shaddad narrates that The Messenger of Allah ﷺ came out to us for one of the nighttime prayers as he was carrying Hasan or Husayn. The Messenger of Allah ﷺ came forward and put him down, then he said "*Allahu akbar*" and started to pray. He prostrated during his prayer, and made the prostration lengthy. The father of the narrator recounts, "I raised my head and saw the child on the back of the Messenger of Allah ﷺ while he was prostrating, so I went back to my prostration." When the Messenger of Allah ﷺ finished praying, the people said: "O Messenger of Allah ﷺ, you prostrated during the prayer for so long that we thought that something had happened, or that you were receiving a revelation." He said: "No such thing happened. My son was riding on my back and I did not like to disturb him until he had enough" (Nasa'i – Sahih).

In another hadith, Abu Qatadah (may allah be pleased with him) narrates:

> We were sitting in the masjid and the Messenger of Allah ﷺ came carrying Umamah bint Abu al-ʿĀs, whose mother was Zaynab, the daughter of the Messenger of Allah ﷺ. He prayed with her on his shoulder and everybody followed in ṣalāh. When he went to *rukooʿ* and *sujood,* he removed her from his shoulder, and when he stood up he put her back on. (Nasa'i – Sahih)

These hadiths tell us that it was common for children to be present at al-Masjid al-Nabawi for ṣalāh. It also tells us the Messenger of Allah ﷺ modified his ṣalāh, shortening it or lengthening it, to accommodate children. The Prophet's ﷺ beautiful example highlights the importance of our masjids being child friendly.

Children can, however, be disruptive. Parents are responsible for teaching their children how to be in the masjid, but it is also the duty of the masjid to accommodate children. Many masjids throughout the United States have game rooms, gymnasiums and specific programs designed for children. Though not every masjid has enough space for these facilities, there could be just a few toys for the children to play with in the back of the prayer space. Another fact to consider is that these disruptive children will soon inherit the masjid when all of the current adults pass on. Instead of constantly reprimanding children, let us welcome them and teach them to love the masjid.

In fact the youth played pivotal roles in Islam. Our beloved Prophet ﷺ paid special attention to the development of the 12 year old Abdullah bin Umar and the 13 year old Abu Ubayda bin al-Jarrah. He ﷺ invested in 16 year olds such as Abdullah bin Masud, Khabbab bin Arat, and Zubayr bin Awwam. It is no surprise then, that each of them became crucial pillars of the Muslim community—may Allah be pleased with them all.

Jundub bin Abdullah (may Allah be pleased with him) narrates, "We were with the Prophet ﷺ while we were strong youths. We learned faith before we learned the Qur'an. Then we learned Qur'an and our faith increased thereby" (Ibn Majah – Sahih). Ali bin Abu Talib (may Allah be pleased with him) became Muslim at the age of ten. He was moved by the message of Islam, which he learned from the Messenger of Allah ﷺ. His faith led him to support Islam publicly when all his uncles, as well as the leaders and noblemen of Mecca, were firmly declaring their opposition to it.

When the Messenger of Allah ﷺ first met Musab bin Umayr and Muadh bin Jabal (may Allah be pleased with him), they were only 18 years old. He ﷺ provided one on one attention to their development, and continuously nurtured their Islamic personality. By these efforts and by the favor of Allah, Musab bin Umayr (may Allah be pleased with him) was later appointed the first ambassador of Islam and Muadh bin Jabal was appointed the first governor of Yemen. Abdullah bin Abbas (may Allah be pleased with him) narrated that the Prophet sent Muadh to Yemen, and said,

> You are going to some of the People of the Book. Call them to bear witness that none has the right to be worshipped but Allah, and that I am the Messenger of Allah. If they oblige, then tell them that Allah has mandated upon them five prayers every day and night. If they oblige, then tell them that Allah has mandated upon them Zakah from their wealth to be taken from the rich and given to their poor. If they oblige, then beware of (taking) the best of their wealth, and beware of the supplication of the oppressed, for there is no barrier between him and Allah. (Ibn Majah – Sahih)

Our beloved Prophet ﷺ would even maximize his time when travelling, regularly taking one of the youth with him to provide them with opportunities to learn from him. The following hadith records a conversation the young Abdullah bin Abbas (may Allah be pleased with him) had with the Prophet ﷺ while he was riding the same animal with him:

> One day I was sitting behind the Messenger of Allah ﷺ on his mount, and he said to me: "Young man, I shall teach you some words [of advice]: Be mindful of Allah, and Allah will protect you. Be mindful of Allah, and you will find Him in front of you. If you ask, ask of Allah; if you seek help, seek help from Allah. Know that if people were to gather together to benefit you with anything, they would only benefit you with what Allah had already prescribed for you; and that if they gather together to harm you with anything, they would only harm you with what Allah had already prescribed for you. The pens have been lifted and the pages have dried." (Tirmidhi–Hassan)

To learn about a hadith like this and then see masjids that do not invest in the youth is a sad rejection of the example of our beloved Prophet ﷺ. Let us ensure our masjids are welcoming to the youth and that it serves their needs.

For the sake of the future of the Muslim ummah, we must make our masjids welcoming to the youth. To that end, we recommend masjids to undertake the following steps:

- Offer play areas and child-care facilities so that little children are entertained when their parents are participating in the masjid.
- Offer formal classes on the basics of Islam (e.g. Weekend school).
- Offer formal classes on Qur'an memorization.
- Offer youth lectures or group study circles for youth of different age ranges.
- Hire a youth director.
- Arrange fun activities for youth (such as swimming, skiing, canoeing, camping, horseback riding, etc.).
- Invest in a gymnasium where youth can play basketball or soccer.
- Install a youth game room with soft seating and other games such as ping pong or billiards.
- Train youth to deliver Jumuʿah sermons at their school or college.
- Provide mentoring opportunities.
- Provide tutoring and homework assistance.
- Organize college admission fairs and career fairs.
- Provide leadership opportunities for young adults.
- Facilitate marriage among the youth.
- Provide pre-marriage and after-marriage counseling.
- Provide new parenting classes.

The Masjid is Welcoming to Women

The Messenger of Allah ﷺ said: "Do not prevent the female servants of Allah from entering the masjid of Allah" (Abu Dawud - Sahih). Yet many of our masjids still fall short in their treatment and accommodation of our sisters. There are many masjids where our sisters are not welcomed, or where their participation is grudgingly tolerated. Many of our sisters feel marginalized and relegated to an afterthought. All this leads to an unwelcoming atmosphere. A wide survey of our female population will show that this experience is commonly shared among them

Since it is ultimately cultural values that drive such unfortunate behavior, we cannot attribute it to Allah the Exalted or to our noble Messenger of Allah ﷺ. Allah the Most High sets the tone of the relationship between Muslim men and women to be one of mutual respect and fairness. He says,

إِنَّ ٱلْمُسْلِمِينَ وَٱلْمُسْلِمَٰتِ وَٱلْمُؤْمِنِينَ وَٱلْمُؤْمِنَٰتِ وَٱلْقَٰنِتِينَ
وَٱلْقَٰنِتَٰتِ وَٱلصَّٰدِقِينَ وَٱلصَّٰدِقَٰتِ وَٱلصَّٰبِرِينَ وَٱلصَّٰبِرَٰتِ
وَٱلْخَٰشِعِينَ وَٱلْخَٰشِعَٰتِ وَٱلْمُتَصَدِّقِينَ وَٱلْمُتَصَدِّقَٰتِ وَٱلصَّٰٓئِمِينَ
وَٱلصَّٰٓئِمَٰتِ وَٱلْحَٰفِظِينَ فُرُوجَهُمْ وَٱلْحَٰفِظَٰتِ وَٱلذَّٰكِرِينَ ٱللَّهَ
كَثِيرًا وَٱلذَّٰكِرَٰتِ أَعَدَّ ٱللَّهُ لَهُم مَّغْفِرَةً وَأَجْرًا عَظِيمًا

Indeed, the Muslim men and Muslim women, the believing men and believing women, the obedient men and obedient women, the truthful men and truthful women, the patient men and patient women, the humble men and humble women, the charitable men and charitable women, the fasting men and fasting women, the men who guard their chastity and the women who do so, and the men who remember Allah often and the women who do so—for them Allah has prepared forgiveness and a great reward. (*Qur'an 33:35*)

Therefore, it is not surprising that women were welcome and fully participatory in al-Masjid al-Nabawi, the perfect exemplary masjid, where the tone of human interaction was set by the model human being: our beloved Prophet Muhammad ﷺ.

The hadith literature documents in extensive detail the regular participation of women in prayer at al-Masjid al-Nabawi. Below we cite only one example, although dozens more exist. Umm Salama (may Allah be pleased with her) said, "Whenever Allah's Messenger ﷺ completed the prayer, the women used to get up immediately and Allah's Messenger ﷺ would remain at his place for some time before getting up." The narrator, Al- Zuhri said that this may have been so that the women could leave before the men, and Allah knows best (Bukhari—Sahih).

Furthermore, the women among the companions used to attend the Fajr prayer in the early morning at al-Masjid al-Nabawi in the dark, without street lights! Arguments about it not being safe, or about needing to take care of the children did not seem to prevent them from praying at the masjid. Again, these are some of the many available hadith demonstrating this point. Aisha (may Allah be pleased with her) narrates that Allah's Messenger ﷺ used to offer the Fajr prayer when it was still dark, and the believing women used to return after finishing their prayer and nobody could recognize them due to the darkness, or they could not recognize one another. (Bukhari—Sahih).

In the generation following the death of the Messenger of Allah ﷺ, the tendency to exclude women arose. Abdullah bin Umar, may Allah be pleased with him, was a senior legal scholar at that time. He was the son of the second Khalifa Umar bin Khattab, may Allah be pleased with him. As a young man, he had spent a lot of time learning from the Messenger of Allah ﷺ. By the time of the following conversation, he was a wise old man, a link for the entire community at the time to the pristine era of the Messenger of Allah ﷺ.

Abdullah bin Umar (may Allah be pleased with him) reported that the Messenger of Allah ﷺ said, "Do not prevent women from going to the mosque at night." A boy said to Abdullah bin Umar, "We would never let them go out, so that they may not be caught in evil." Abdullah bin Umar reprimanded him and said, "I am telling you the Messenger of Allah ﷺ said this, but then you say: 'We would not allow'?!" (Muslim—Sahih). Any arguments to prevent women from the masjid have been defeated over a thousand years ago!

We sometimes hear the argument that women should not go to crowded places with many people out of a sense of modesty or privacy. Our beloved Prophet ﷺ went out of his way to ensure that women were included in the community celebrations and Eid prayers that were held in public spaces outside the masjid. The Messenger of Allah ﷺ said: "Bring out the women who have attained puberty and those who are in seclusion so that they may attend the Eid prayer and the supplication of the Muslims" (Ibn Majah—Sahih).

Some advocate prioritizing the needs of the men in the community over the women, especially when resources are scarce. They use this type of argument to justify not investing in or maintaining the facilities that are used by women. They cite the fact that women are not required to attend Jumuʿah prayers to avoid installing new carpets in the women's section or even expanding the men's section at the expense of the women's. Attitudes and actions like these make our sisters feel marginalized and neglected.

Jabir bin Abdullah (may Allah be pleased with him) narrates a hadith that demonstrates how the Messenger of Allah ﷺ made sure that women were invited to the community events, and also that they received religious services, even on the most important day of Eid:

> I attended the prayer with the Messenger of Allah ﷺ on the day of Eid. He started with the prayer before the khutba, with no adhan and no iqamah. When he finished the prayer, he stood up, lean-

> ing on Bilal, and he praised and glorified Allah and exhorted the people, reminding them and urging them to obey Allah . Then he moved away and went to the women, and Bilal came with him. He commanded them to fear Allah, exhorted them and reminded them. He praised and glorified Allah, then he urged them to obey Allah. (Nasa'i—Sahih)

The participation of the women companions at al-Masjid al-Nabawi was routine and matter of fact. His concern for the often overlooked sectors of society was remarkable for the culture of his time.

Another hadith demonstrates the Prophet's small, but thoughtful, gestures to help everyone in the community feel welcomed. He ﷺ passed through the masjid one day when a group of women were sitting, and he motioned his hand to greet them (Tirmidhi—Hassan). These hadith, in addition to many others, describe in great detail how the women had regular access to the Messenger of Allah ﷺ, in order to learn from him and voice their concerns to him. When they felt their access limited, they even asserted themselves and asked for special time, which was readily granted. Abu Said Al-Khudri narrated that some women requested the Prophet ﷺ to set a day for them, as the men were taking all his time. On that he promised them one day for teaching them religious lessons and commandments. Once during such a lesson the Prophet said, "A woman whose three children die will be shielded by them from the Hell fire.» A woman asked, "What if only two die?» He replied, "Even two" (Bukhari—Sahih).

Aishah even pointed out how keen the women from Medina were to inquire about even the most sensitive matters. She praised them, saying, "The best women are the women of the Ansar. Shyness would not prevent them from inquiring about religion and from acquiring deep understanding in it" (Abu Dawud—Hasan). The idea that shyness or modesty should prevent Muslim women from learning and accessing the masjid is foreign to our tradition. It is nothing more than a product of our cultural bias and other factors alien to Islam.

We mentioned in an earlier chapter the hadith of the woman who perfumed the al-Masjid al-Nabawi. In another hadith, we learn about a woman who took ownership of the masjid and regularly cleaned it. Abu Hurairah narrated that a black woman used to sweep the masjid. The Messenger of Allah ﷺ noticed she was missing and he asked about her after a few days. When he was told that she had died, he said: "Why did you not tell me?"

Then he went to her grave and offered the funeral prayer for her (Ibn Majah—Sahih).

Because she was not a local, some companions may have assumed that this woman's death might not be significant to the Messenger of Allah ﷺ. He, however, saw the matter very differently. He considered her a part of the masjid community. He considered her someone deserving of his personal presence at her funeral due to her participation and belonging to the masjid. Since he missed her funeral prayer, he made a point of going to her grave and praying for her even after she was buried.

Not only did the women companions regularly attend al-Masjid al-Nabawi, they participated in decision making activities also. In the following incident, the women were having a hard time seeing the Messenger of Allah ﷺ during his sermons because of the distance. One of the women took it upon herself to propose a solution for the problem. The pulpit, now the symbol of religious authority in Islam, was sponsored and commissioned by a woman in response to the needs of her fellow worshippers. Dozens of narrations exist in the hadith literature for this incident. Other narrations describe the pulpit was constructed with three steps and also describe the day it was installed and first used, noting its landmark status in the history of the Ummah.

Jabir bin Abdullah (may Allah be pleased with him) narrated that an Ansari woman said to Allah's Messenger ﷺ, "Allah's Messenger ﷺ, Shall I make something for you to sit on as I have a slave who is a carpenter." He replied, "If you wish." She had a pulpit made for him, and when it was Friday, the Prophet ﷺ sat on that pulpit (Bukhari—Sahih).

Many masjid goers and even members of administration are deeply offended by the thought of women entering the main prayer hall. The following hadith narrated by Asma bint Abu Bakr shows how the men and women listened to a lecture in the same room, such that the women and men could talk to each other:

> The Messenger of Allah stood up and mentioned the trial with which a person will be tested in his grave. When he mentioned that, the people became restless, which prevented me from understanding what the Messenger of Allah had said. When they settled down, I said to a man who was near me: "May Allah bless you—what did he say at the end?" He said: "It has been revealed to me that you will be tested in your graves with a trial close to that of the Dajjal." (Nasa'i – Sahih)

Abdullah bin Umar describes how the companions persevered in their Islamic duties, even when the masjid did not have separate wudu' facilities for men and women.

He said, "During the lifetime of Allah's Messenger ﷺ men and women used to perform ablution together" (Bukhari—Sahih). No one is asking for men and women to do wudu' together, this hadith and others like it are useful in helping us understand that we do not need to create such isolating boundaries between men and women in the masjid.

Our pious predecessors, the model generations of the companions of Allah's Messenger ﷺ and those who succeeded them, did not have a problem with women who were deeply involved in Islamic work. They readily accepted the idea of women teaching men and men teaching women. The notable scholar of hadith, Shaykh Mohammad Akram Nadwi recently completed an exhaustive 40 volume analysis on the women scholars of Hadith (*muḥaddithāt*) across 1400 years and all throughout the Muslim lands. His study includes exhaustive analysis of over 8,000 *muhaddithāt*. Only the introduction to this study has been published in English so far.

He identified almost 2,000 women Companions who narrated hadith. Of them 130 are recorded in the most authoritative Six Books of hadith. Imam Bukhari lists 31 female Companions of Allah's Messenger ﷺ, Imam Muslim 36, Imam Abu Dawud 75, Imam Tirmidhi 46, Imam Nasa'i 65, and Imam ibn Majah 60. The analysis also identified almost 1,200 female students of Companions, of whom 130 are recorded in the Six Books. Shaykh Mohammad Akram Nadwi says:

> There is no period when men have certain privileges to speak or think or act, and then women find a way to "invade" the men's ground. Rather the women and the men both know, from the outset of Islam, what their duties are ... There is no evidence of any campaign, overt or covert, to win rights from men for women.

He goes on to describe the sixth to the ninth centuries of the Islamic calendar as "*the brightest period in the history of the muḥaddithāt*". He says, "*from the sixth century, their numbers grow rapidly, peaking in the eighth, beginning to go down in the ninth.*"

The hadith and historical record makes clear that women have played dynamic roles in the Muslim community until approximately 500 years ago. Concurrent with the arrival of European colonialism in Muslim lands, a sharp decline in the participation of women can be seen. While we suspect a causal connection between the two, we have not been able to document that from scholarly analysis.

Allah says,

وَٱلْمُؤْمِنُونَ وَٱلْمُؤْمِنَٰتُ بَعْضُهُمْ أَوْلِيَآءُ بَعْضٍ يَأْمُرُونَ بِٱلْمَعْرُوفِ وَيَنْهَوْنَ عَنِ ٱلْمُنكَرِ وَيُقِيمُونَ ٱلصَّلَوٰةَ وَيُؤْتُونَ ٱلزَّكَوٰةَ وَيُطِيعُونَ ٱللَّهَ وَرَسُولَهُۥٓ أُو۟لَٰٓئِكَ سَيَرْحَمُهُمُ ٱللَّهُ إِنَّ ٱللَّهَ عَزِيزٌ حَكِيمٌ

The believing men and believing women are allies of one another. They promote good and forbid evil, and establish prayer, and give Zakah, and obey Allah and His Messenger. Upon them Allah will have mercy. Indeed, Allah is Exalted in Might and Wise. (*Qur'an 9:71*)

This ayah teaches us that it is of urgent importance to the Muslim community to make our masjids welcoming to women. To that end, we recommend masjids undertake the following steps:

- Women who attend regular prayers every day have a right to dignified accommodations, ideally in the main prayer hall.
- If a separate prayer hall is designated for women, it must be of similar quality as the prayer hall for men. It should have windows, lights, clean carpeting, and air conditioning similar to the main hall. It must not be constructed as an afterthought. Ensure the sound system is fully functional to provide proper services.
- Some women need or prefer greater privacy. In places where women have access to the main prayer hall, provide means of privacy for such women.
- Women who attend Friday prayers have a right to dignified accommodations, ideally in the main prayer hall.
- If the masjid has a separate entrance for women, it should be safe and well lit.
- Donation boxes should be accessible to women.
- Electronic display screens and announcement boards should be accessible to women.
- Regular education programs should be available for women of all ages and address a wide range of topics (not just "female" issues).
- Offer play areas and child-care facilities so that women with children are not prevented from participation.

These should not be seen as a favor from the men in the community to the women. These steps should be undertaken to fulfill the affirmative right of the Muslim women to worship their Lord, just like men. They are human beings created by Allah and endowed with honor and dignity by Allah. If the above fails to convince someone, then we offer one last perspective: how can a society develop if half the population is denied the opportunity to contribute to its growth?

The famous scholar and teacher, Imam Ibn Qayyim al-Jawziyyah said, "Women are one half of society who give birth to the other half. So it is as if they are the entire society." The average Muslim learns their love of Allah and the basics of their religion from their mothers. What will be the future of the ummah without our mothers as the guardians of the faith? Let us make the masjid welcoming to women.

Welcoming New Muslims

Most companions of Prophet Muhammad ﷺ were new Muslims, and so they had a clearly marked transition date when they entered Islam. They interacted with family members who were not Muslims on a daily basis and dealt with hostility, rejection, and lack of awareness from everyone around them. Their struggles with their environment was made even more challenging by the internal pains of being alone. Nowadays most Muslims are born into Muslim families, which is an immense blessing, but hinders our understanding of the unique challenges faced by new Muslims.

Like the Companions (may Allah be pleased with them), new Muslims face unique challenges. There is a deep gap in knowledge between what the Muslims who grow up in Muslim families take as common knowledge and the information that is readily available for new Muslims to learn. Often they feel shy to ask the simple questions such as the specific steps of prayer or the rules of fasting. A misplaced sense of shame or shyness might drive them to refrain from asking questions, which is why we may find someone who has been Muslim for a long period of time, but still doesn't know a detail as simple as the words for tashahhud, which those of us who grew up praying learned at a young age.

New Muslims also deal with loneliness that can be sometimes crippling. Many new Muslims don't have friends who invite them for Eid or Iftar. They may not have a large group of friends who can be with them and help them celebrate their marriage or advise and support them through the challenges of everyday life. Many new Muslims continue to struggle with burdensome remnants of their previous lives. These could include estranged family ties, financial issues, or even legal issues.

We often don't realize these difficulties that our new Muslim brothers and sisters experience. We must proactively identify ways to ease that pain and offer an inclusive environment that is crucial for maintaining faith. It is our duty to make our masjids welcoming to new Muslims. For this we make the following recommendations:

- Establish a New Muslim Support Group.
- Establish a New Muslim Study Circle.
- Provide educational materials on every major topic. Giving out copies of the Qur'an is not enough. They need materials teaching them how to pray, fast, perform purification rituals, pay zakat, etc.
- Whenever a person accepts Islam in the masjid, assign them a mentor with more knowledge who is willing to be available for him or her.
- Protect the new Muslim from being criticized for small mistakes they make simply because they may not know all the rules. It is going to take some time for them to adapt to all of the rules of Islam. Our religion has a field of study that analyzes which rules are to be given the most attention first; it's called the Rules of Priorities (*fiqh al-awlawiyyāt*).
- Protect the new Muslim from the cultural expectations of the other attendees of the masjid. The new Muslim does not need to follow Arab, Desi, or any other foreign cultural expectations.
- The new Muslim does NOT need to change their name unless their name has an offensive meaning.

Getting this right is very important to the Muslim ummah. Islam is the fastest growing religion, but a large percentage of Muslims leave Islam daily. One Pew Research study sheds light on this issue:

> About a quarter of adults who were raised Muslim (23%) no longer identify as members of the faith, roughly on par with the share of Americans who were raised Christian and no longer identify with Christianity (22%), according to a new analysis of the 2014 Religious Landscape Study. But while the share of American Muslim adults who are converts to Islam also is about one-quarter (23%), a much smaller share of current Christians (6%) are converts. In other words, Christianity as a whole loses more people than it gains from religious switching (conversions in both directions) in the U.S., while the net effect on Islam in America is a wash.

For the future of the ummah, we must integrate our new brothers and sisters into our community.

Catering To Disabled Muslims

All people, including Muslims with disabilities, are human beings endowed with dignity by Allah. Allah says,

وَلَقَدْ كَرَّمْنَا بَنِيٓ ءَادَمَ وَحَمَلْنَٰهُمْ فِى ٱلْبَرِّ وَٱلْبَحْرِ وَرَزَقْنَٰهُم مِّنَ ٱلطَّيِّبَٰتِ وَفَضَّلْنَٰهُمْ عَلَىٰ كَثِيرٍ مِّمَّنْ خَلَقْنَا تَفْضِيلًا

And We have certainly honored the children of Adam, and carried them on the land and sea, and provided for them good things, and preferred them over much of what We have created with [definite] preference. (*Qur'an 17:70*)

Asserting the importance of supporting and assisting the disabled, the Messenger of Allah ﷺ said: "Cursed is he who misleads a blind person away from his path" (Ahmad – Hassan). As such, Muslims with disabilities have an affirmative right to worship their Lord and participate in the civic life of the Muslim community. Unfortunately a small number of masjid administrators consider the requirements of the American with Disabilities Act (ADA) to be a nuisance.

The Prophet ﷺ also said: "Seek out the weak among you on my behalf. Indeed you are provided sustenance and victory by virtue of the weak among you" (Tirmidhi, Abu Dawud – Sahih). Some masjids have steep stairs with no wheelchair ramp. Some even lack a handrail. The ablution area is often tiled and slippery. Deaf Muslims feel left out of the Friday sermon, lectures, classes or other gatherings due to a lack of sign language interpreters. It is rare to find a Qur'an in braille for vision-impaired Muslims.

As able bodied people, most of us do not appreciate the great bounty Allah has provided us and we often don't realize the challenges our handicapped Muslim brothers and sisters face on a day to day basis. It is our duty to make our masjids welcoming to handicapped Muslims. We make the following recommendations for this:

- Comply with all provisions of the American with Disabilities Act (ADA).
- Install signage for handicapped parking spots conveniently close to the entrance of the masjid.
- Ensure the handicapped parking spots are not being misused by people not eligible to use such spots.
- Install wheelchair ramps or wheelchair lifts wherever stairs exist. The ramps should not be steep. Follow local building codes in this regard.

The gradient should not exceed 1:12 even if the local building codes permit steep ramps.

- Install railings on wheelchair ramps & stairs.
- Install railings and slip guard strips on the floors in bathrooms and wuduʾ areas.
- Provide sign language interpreters wherever financially possible.
- Provide Qur'ans in braille.
- Maintain a bulletin board for congregants.

The masjid should be welcoming to the entire community. If there is a wedding, for example, it should be in the masjid. If the family is happy because their child graduated, that should happen in the masjid, and if they are sorrowful because someone died, then that should happen in the masjid where people come and share the pain with them. That is how it was at al-Masjid al-Nabawi. In the spirit of making the masjid a center for community engagement, the Institute for Social Policy and Understanding makes the following recommendations to make a masjid more welcoming:

- Form a Welcoming Committee.
- Create a welcoming culture.
- Nurture a safe environment.
- Organize activities at which people get to know one another.
- Provide welcoming packets for newcomers.
- Facilitate socializing and developing friendships.
- Install good signage.
- Organize a Wellness Committee.
- Embrace diversity.
- Improve communication.
- Listen to the community.

Let us make our masjids follow the template of the ideal we all strive to emulate: al-Masjid al-Nabawi.

Chapter 7: The Daʿwah Center

The masjid of the Messenger of Allah ﷺ was the center for daʿwah. It welcomed people exploring Islam inside and introduced them to Islam. The Messenger of Allah ﷺ met people of other faiths in his masjid and thousands of them embraced Islam. Al-Masjid al-Nabawi was originally very small before the expansions made to it after the Prophet's ﷺ death. Many masjid administrators mistakenly assume that they cannot do daʿwah because their masjid is small, but we learn from the Prophet's model that the size of the masjid is not relevant to its impact and benefit on its surrounding community.

Every election season, various politicians decide to attack Islam and Muslims as a means to political success. Hardly a day goes by without an attack against Islam or Muslims. This is the core of Islamophobia. But it is not new; it also existed during the time of the Messenger ﷺ. The Qur'an refers to it as preventing people from the path of Allah (*sadd an sabilillah*).

We have a duty to respond to it. Imam Ibn al-Qayyim points out that whenever Allah, the Most High, wishes to honor a group of people, he brings forth on the earth people who will attack His religion. Then He allows the former to stand out and defend it against the latter, thereby attaining honor and dignity in the eyes of God and His creation.

Though the enemies of Islam are attacking it, eventually Allah's master plan will be implemented. During the Salman Rushdie issue of the 1980s, some said Islam was barbaric, worthless, and backwards. People also commented that Muslims do not have a sense of humor and do not understand the concept of freedom of speech. A Muslim who lived in England during this controversy described how every week people came to his masjid to embrace Islam.

The same pattern repeated in the United States. After September 11, 2001, the situation deteriorated rapidly for Muslims. However, with the passage of time, we are now able to step back and look at the big picture, seeing that a large number of people entered Islam even after that tragic event.

The enemies of Allah attack Islam seeking to hurt it. They spend millions in their attempt but Allah is the master planner and He has His own plans. A part of His plan is that He will bring something good despite their attacks on Islam and He will do so through the efforts of the enemies of Islam. He says,

إِنَّ ٱلَّذِينَ كَفَرُوا يُنفِقُونَ أَمْوَٰلَهُمْ لِيَصُدُّوا عَن سَبِيلِ ٱللَّهِ فَسَيُنفِقُونَهَا ثُمَّ تَكُونُ عَلَيْهِمْ حَسْرَةً ثُمَّ يُغْلَبُونَ وَٱلَّذِينَ كَفَرُوٓا إِلَىٰ جَهَنَّمَ يُحْشَرُونَ

Indeed, the disbelievers spend their wealth to avert people from the way of Allah. So they will spend it; then it will be for them a source of regret; then they will be defeated. And they will be gathered in Hell in their disbelief. (*Qur'an 8:36*)

Allah, the All Powerful arranges amazing outcomes from horrible events. This is part of Allah's master plan. Then Allah, the Most Wise, explains our role in this master plan:

وَلَا تَسْتَوِى ٱلْحَسَنَةُ وَلَا ٱلسَّيِّئَةُ ٱدْفَعْ بِٱلَّتِى هِىَ أَحْسَنُ فَإِذَا ٱلَّذِى بَيْنَكَ وَبَيْنَهُۥ عَدَٰوَةٌ كَأَنَّهُۥ وَلِىٌّ حَمِيمٌ

Good and evil are not alike. Respond to evil with good and your enemy can become your dear friend. (*Qur'an 41:34*)

Then Allah, the Exalted, gives a subtle warning about this matter. This action, repelling evil with good, is not easy; most people cannot do it. None can do it except those who have patience and none other than those can do it accept the ones who have been favored by Allah. And so Allah says,

وَمَا يُلَقَّىٰهَآ إِلَّا ٱلَّذِينَ صَبَرُوا وَمَا يُلَقَّىٰهَآ إِلَّا ذُو حَظٍّ عَظِيمٍ

But none can accomplish this except the patient, who are greatly favored by Allah. (*Qur'an 41:35*)

Let's analyze this verse in the context of our reality: A large group of people want to deport Muslims. Some people even want to attack the Kaaba. There are sick individuals who wish to vandalize every neighborhood masjid and harm their congregants. And while groups advocating for "freedom of speech" continuously attack our beloved Prophet Muhammad ﷺ, our hearts hurt! Yet Allah teaches us to respond to these terrorizing threats with patience and kindness to distinguish our standards from theirs. When they go low, we go high.

If some people burn the Qur'an, we should not go out and burn a Bible in revenge; that is forbidden! The Muslim response to somebody burning the Qur'an should be to print two more Qur'ans and give it to two more people!

When they burn one, I will replace it with two. That is following Allah's instructions in the Qur'an to respond with what is better.

This brings us to the broader idea of the duty of daʿwah belonging to the entire Muslim community after the death of our beloved Prophet ﷺ. Whereas this responsibility was exclusive to the prophets, the Messenger of Allah ﷺ taught us that it was now our duty to spread the message of Islam in the most beautiful way. Allah highlights this as our distinction as a nation throughout history:

خَيْرَ أُمَّةٍ أُخْرِجَتْ لِلنَّاسِ تَأْمُرُونَ بِٱلْمَعْرُوفِ وَتَنْهَوْنَ عَنِ ٱلْمُنكَرِ وَتُؤْمِنُونَ بِٱللَّهِ

"You are the best nation of humanity because you promote what is right and forbid what is wrong and believe in Allah." (*Qur'an 3:110*)

In this verse, Allah the Exalted describes us, the followers of Prophet Muhammad ﷺ as the "best of nations." But this quality is only actualized when we fulfill the conditions mentioned with it: 1) promoting good, 2) forbidding evil, and 3) believing in Allah. When we perfect these three things, we can be the best of nations

In addition to this incentive, our Lord affirmatively commands:

ٱدْعُ إِلَىٰ سَبِيلِ رَبِّكَ بِٱلْحِكْمَةِ وَٱلْمَوْعِظَةِ ٱلْحَسَنَةِ وَجَٰدِلْهُم بِٱلَّتِي هِيَ أَحْسَنُ

"Call to the path of your Lord with wisdom, good speech, and debate with them in the most courteous way." (*Qur'an 16:125*)

قُلْ هَٰذِهِۦ سَبِيلِىٓ أَدْعُوٓا۟ إِلَى ٱللَّهِ عَلَىٰ بَصِيرَةٍ أَنَا۠ وَمَنِ ٱتَّبَعَنِى

"Say, 'This is my path; I and those who follow me call unto Allah insightfully.'" (*Qur'an 12:108*)

The Prophet ﷺ said, "Convey (my teachings) to the people even if it were a single sentence." (Bukhari, Tirmidhi)

The point we should take from the above is that the duty of daʿwah is not restricted to the prophets, it is not restricted to the Companions, and it is not restricted to the scholars; it is a duty of the broad spectrum and belongs to the entirety of the Ummah. We do not find in the Qur'an, a statement where Allah only commands the scholars to pray. Rather it is mandatory for everyone. Similarly, this duty of daʿwah belongs to you and me.

When considering the power of daʿwah, we should realize that more than half of all Americans do not believe what they hear about Muslims even after twenty years of Islamophobic content in the media. The hateful and unjust portrayal of Islam in the media could be counterbalanced by just one pleasant interaction with a Muslim. When they see Muslims bringing peace and benefit to the communities around them, they have no choice but to believe their own personal experiences over the misrepresentation of the religion. That's the power of individual human interactions.

Every masjid has a duty to become a daʿwah powerhouse. Some ideas for a masjid to participate in:

- Muslim Day at the Capitol
- State or county fair Daʿwah Booth
- Ramadan Iftar Open House
- Masjid Open House Day
- Know Your Muslim Neighbor events
- Interfaith Service Projects

We all have a role in daʿwah. Ali bin Abu Talib (may Allah be pleased with him) participated in daʿwah when he was ten years old, proving that no member of the community is unable to take part in the project of teaching and spreading Islam. Boxer Muhammad Ali suffered from Parkinson's disease, and was extremely weak in the last two years of his life. His hands would shake ceaselessly, and he was unable to walk. Yet in his very last days, he would still use all the energy he had to sign educational pamphlets about Islam. When asked why he chose to sign these documents over other more symbolic artifacts, he said that if you give this document to any average person who is not Muslim and say that it is signed by Muhammad Ali, they would never throw it away. The probability that they would actually read it would increase simply because it is autographed by Muhammad Ali. He decided to use his greatest asset, his reputation, to promote Islam!

A common obstacle to daʿwah is not being confident in one's own religious knowledge. But there are many examples of people finding Islam through laymen who exemplified prophetic character, rather than some scholar who had an answer for every question. A brother told us how he became a Muslim: While studying at university, he would do assignments and homework with his Muslim classmate who could not speak English well. When he suggested they meet on Friday afternoon, his classmate said that he could not meet since he had to attend "Jumuʿah." Curious to know what this was, he asked for more details, and when his classmate's English skills failed to convey the concept clearly, he requested to attend in order to observe. He recounted that what stood out most to him was the equality of the all people in front of God when they stood in prayer, and he became a Muslim that very day. Here is an example of a man who could not speak proper English but still strove for daʿwah.

Allah The Exalted commanded us and encouraged us as follows.

وَمَنْ أَحْسَنُ قَوْلًا مِّمَّن دَعَآ إِلَى ٱللَّهِ وَعَمِلَ صَـٰلِحًا وَقَالَ إِنَّنِى مِنَ ٱلْمُسْلِمِينَ

And who is better in speech than one who calls to Allah, acts righteously, and says, "Indeed, I am of the Muslims?" (Qur'an 41:33)

This lofty position can be attained by you and me. The examples above show us that there is no pre-required condition for sharing the message of Islam. Brothers and sisters with far less of an education have had great impacts on their local communities. We have no excuse.

In the midst of all of this, we should remember always that our duty is to convey, not to convert. In fact, Allah told His Messenger ﷺ that it is only Allah who gives guidance, despite the Prophet ﷺ being the best preacher and teacher to ever walk the earth. This was made clear when the Prophet ﷺ could not convince his uncle, who had raised him, protected him, and supported him throughout his campaign, to renounce the pagan religion of his forefathers. Our primary concern in daʿwah should be to convey the message in the best possible manner in order to first exonerate ourselves of any blame. This includes speaking nicely, and politely, answering questions gently and clearing up misconceptions wisely.

Success is not measured by counting the number of people who convert to Islam at our hands. We often celebrate at the event of someone publicly declaring their entrance into the religion with the testimony of faith, but forget the events and efforts that led up to it. I used to be in contact with someone who was curious and interested in learning more about Islam because of an English copy of the Qur'an that someone had gifted her thirty years ago; she had let it collect dust on the shelf before picking it up decades later to begin her journey for the truth. We may not see the results of our efforts immediately,—or even at all—but it is important to always remember the potential impact of even the smallest gestures.

This attitude applies to all of our efforts to spread the religion and improve our communities. Taking this book as an example, I should hope that by sharing these thoughts, I am firstly fulfilling my duty to the Muslim community in the sight of Allah. My goal is not to force these suggestions onto any person or institution, but rather to promote a higher standard of engagement and values for our communities. The result is in the hands of Allah.

Lastly, we must realize our collective duty to undertake this effort. There is no one else who can perform this task for us. It is our responsibility to defend our own religion and speak for ourselves against Islamophobic efforts to redefine Islam, working hard to define it ourselves through action and education.

Chapter 8: Mercy To Humanity

Our master and teacher Muhammad ﷺ was described by the Lord of all the worlds, Glorified and Exalted, with the most beautiful description.

وَمَآ أَرْسَلْنَٰكَ إِلَّا رَحْمَةً لِّلْعَٰلَمِينَ

And We have not sent you, [O Muhammad], except as a mercy to all the worlds. (Qur'an 21:107)

In one of the most famous and widespread reports, the Messenger of Allah ﷺ said: "Show mercy to those on earth, and He Who is in the heavens (i.e. Allah) will bestow mercy upon you" (Abu Dawud – Sahih).

The masjid of the Messenger of Allah ﷺ functioned in part as a social service agency. One of the earliest actions undertaken by the Messenger of Allah ﷺ in his masjid is establishing Al-Ṣuffah, which served as a shelter and resource for people who would today be considered immigrants and refugees. Abu Hurairah reported: I saw seventy of the people of the Ṣuffah, and none of them had a cloak. They had either a lower garment or a blanket which they suspended from their necks. Some garments reached halfway down to the legs and some to the ankles, and the men would hold it to avoid exposing himself (Bukhari – Sahih).

The Prophet ﷺ had so much concern for these Muslims that He even opened his own home to them. Yaish bin Qais bin Tikhfah narrated that his father, who was one of the people of Suffah, said: "The Messenger of Allah said to us: 'Come with me.' So we went to the house of Aishah, where we ate and drank. Then the Messenger of Allah said to us: 'If you want, you can sleep here, or if you want you can go out to the masjid.' We said: 'We will go out to the masjid'" (Ibn Majah – Sahih). These hadith demonstrate how al-Masjid al-Nabawi was used as a shelter for underserved populations, most of whom were utterly destitute. Abu Hurayrah (may Allah be pleased with him) narrates in another hadith to demonstrate this point:

> The people of As-Suffah were the guests of the people of Islam. They had no people or wealth to rely upon. And By Allah, other than Whom there is none worthy of worship, I would lay on the ground on my side due to hunger, fastening a stone to my stomach because of it. One day I sat by the path the Companions used to exit from. Abu Bakr passed by and I asked him about an ayah from Allah's Book, only asking him so that he might tell me to follow him for

something to eat. But he passed on without doing so. Then Umar passed, so I asked him about an ayah from Allah's Book, only asking him so that he might tell me to follow him. But he passed on without doing so. Then Abul-Qasim ﷺ passed by. He smiled when he saw me, and said: "Abu Hurairah?" I said: "I am here O Messenger of Allah!" He said: "Come along." He continued on and I followed him. He entered his house, so I sought permission to enter, and he permitted me. He found a bowl of milk and said: "Where did this milk come from?" Someone said: "It was a gift to us from so–and–so." Then the Messenger of Allah ﷺ said: "O Abu Hurairah" I said: "I am here, Messenger of Allah!" He said: "Go to the people of Al-Ṣuffah to invite them." They were the guests of the people of Islam, they had no people or wealth to rely upon. Whenever some charity was brought to him, he would send it to them without using any of it. And when a gift was given to him ﷺ, he would send for them to participate and share with him in it.

I became upset about that, and I said to myself: "What good will this bowl be among all the people of Al-Ṣuffah, and I am the one bringing it to them?" Then he ordered me to circulate it among them. So I wondered how much of it would reach me from it, and I hoped that I would get from it enough to satisfy me. But I would certainly not neglect to obey Allah and obey His Messenger, so I went to them and invited them. When they entered, they sat down. He said: "Abu Hurairah, take the bowl and give it to them." So I gave it to a man who drank his fill, then he gave it to another one, until it ended up with the Messenger of Allah ﷺ after all of the people had drunk their fill. The Messenger of Allah ﷺ took the bowl, put it on his hand, and then raised his head. He smiled and said: 'Abu Hurairah, drink,' so I drank. Then he said again: 'Drink.' I kept drinking and he kept on saying, 'Drink.' Then I said: 'By the One Who sent you with the truth! I have no more space for it.' So he took the bowl, praised Allah, mentioned His name and drank." (Tirmidhi - Sahih)

This hadith is one of hundreds that demonstrates the use of al-Masjid al-Nabawi as a social service agency. Thus it is no surprise that the orphanages and *awqāf* of the Muslim communities grew out of masjids.

The first clinic in the Muslim world evolved out of the masjid. The hospital of Ibn Sina, the great father of Muslim medicine, grew out of his masjid. Most people do not know that he was actually a religious scholar who wrote books on theology and religious law. Classically, a masjid would choose one particular field to provide services in. While one, like al-Azhar, focused its efforts in education and knowledge, another might have been known to offer medical services or charity in the form of food. For us to diminish the masjid's role to a prayer space only is a failure to uphold the tradition and heritage through which we have attained such greatness.

When a Muslim group in America approaches a city desiring to build a masjid, local opposition is predictable and loud. People are averse to the thought of a masjid in their neighborhood because of the "problems" usually associated with the existence of a masjid. If a masjid were to carry the reputation of community service and concern for its neighbors, people will begin to advocate for masjids to be built in their neighborhood, and our efforts would be impervious to the inevitable attacks from Islamophobic opposition.

Chapter 9: The Green Masjid

People assume that discussing the environment is somehow a western or modern concept, disconnected from Islam. A closer and more comprehensive look at Islamic teachings will prove this to be far from true. We are concerned for the wellbeing and preservation of the earth and everything upon it because of our devotion and obedience to its Creator and Owner. Allah the Exalted explains:

يُسَبِّحُ لِلَّهِ مَا فِى ٱلسَّمَٰوَٰتِ وَمَا فِى ٱلْأَرْضِ ٱلْمَلِكِ ٱلْقُدُّوسِ ٱلْعَزِيزِ ٱلْحَكِيمِ

"Whatever is in the heavens and whatever is in the earth is praising Allah, the Sovereign, the Pure, the Exalted in Might, the Wise." (Qur'an 62:1)

Further, He the Exalted explicitly claims total and complete ownership of everything:

لَهُۥ مَا فِى ٱلسَّمَٰوَٰتِ وَمَا فِى ٱلْأَرْضِ وَمَا بَيْنَهُمَا وَمَا تَحْتَ ٱلثَّرَىٰ

"To Allah belongs whatever is in the heavens and whatever in the land and whatever between the earth and the heavens and whatever is under the soil." (Qur'an 20:6)

The concept that everything belongs to Allah is mentioned in the Qur'an over twenty times. Secular and materialist influences cause people to see the forest, the mountain, the land, the river and the sea as if they don't have an owner, leading them to feel free to do whatever they want. But Allah has the right to determine how His property is to be treated. He also clarifies that He continues to monitor the condition of His property. Allah, the Supreme, declares:

لَّهُۥ مَا فِى ٱلسَّمَٰوَٰتِ وَمَا فِى ٱلْأَرْضِ وَكَفَىٰ بِٱللَّهِ وَكِيلًا

To Allah belongs whatever in the heavens and the earth and Allah is sufficient to be the disposer of these affairs. (Qur'an 4:171)

Allah also says:

وَلَقَدْ خَلَقْنَا فَوْقَكُمْ سَبْعَ طَرَآئِقَ وَمَا كُنَّا عَنِ ٱلْخَلْقِ غَٰفِلِينَ

"And We did indeed create above you seven mighty ones and We are not unaware of our creation." (Qur'an 23:17)

Taking care of the environment is deeply rooted in Islam. Allah the Exalted describes the creation of our father Adam ﷺ. He said to the angels before creating him:

وَإِذْ قَالَ رَبُّكَ لِلْمَلَٰٓئِكَةِ إِنِّى جَاعِلٌ فِى ٱلْأَرْضِ خَلِيفَةً

"And when your Lord said to the angels, 'Indeed, I will make upon the earth a steward.'" (Qur'an 2:30)

The word *khalīfah* has two meanings. The first meaning is to be a steward, guardian, or caretaker, as shown above. And the second meaning comes from the word "Khalaf" which alludes to the future successive generations. Both meanings are correct, and so this ayah alludes to not just Adam (peace be upon him) who came to the earth as steward, but it is also a word to describe him and his successive generations. This is Allah's master plan.

Allah the Exalted explains:

وَهُوَ ٱلَّذِى جَعَلَكُمْ خَلَٰٓئِفَ ٱلْأَرْضِ وَرَفَعَ بَعْضَكُمْ فَوْقَ بَعْضٍ دَرَجَٰتٍ

"And He is the one who made you successors upon this land and has raised some of you above others in degrees." (Qur'an 6:165)

Islam doesn't prevent us from using natural resources, as Allah permitted us and encouraged us to seek and utilize His bounties. Many people are confused as to whether we are even allowed to benefit from the labor of horses and bees? Some even go as far as criticizing the consumption of meat and milk. Islam's beauty lies in its balanced approach to these issues, permitting us to utilize the world around us for our own benefit, while respecting the rights of the creatures and earth around us. Islam protects us from both extremes: that of abusing and harming the environment, and that of depriving ourselves of natural sources of nourishment.

Allah, the Exalted, commanded us not to waste:

يَٰبَنِىٓ ءَادَمَ خُذُوا۟ زِينَتَكُمْ عِندَ كُلِّ مَسْجِدٍ وَكُلُوا۟ وَٱشْرَبُوا۟ وَلَا تُسْرِفُوٓا۟ إِنَّهُۥ لَا يُحِبُّ ٱلْمُسْرِفِينَ

"O children of Adam, take your beautiful things to every masjid and eat and drink but don't commit excess, because Allah doesn't love those who commit excess." (Qur'an 7:31)

This ayah was revealed in relation to a particular problem. Most of the Muhājiroon who came from Mecca to Medina were very poor because they were forced to leave behind their wealth. Because of this, they would dress in the only clothes they had, which would sometimes be old and worn out. The Anṣār were new Muslims who took the newly arrived immigrants to Medina as their teachers in religion. Although they had better clothes, the Anṣār started wearing shabby clothes to emulate their teachers. This verse was revealed to clarify that Islam is a religion of balance.

ʿAmr bin Shuʿayb narrates from his father, who narrates from his grandfather, that a bedouin man came to the Prophet ﷺ and asked him about ablution. He showed him how to perform it washing each part of the body three times. Then he said: "This is the ablution, and whoever does more than this, has done evil, transgressed the limits, and wronged himself" (Ibn Majah – Hassan).

There are many hadiths that describe the Messenger of Allah ﷺ performing wudu' by washing his hands and face and feet one time, and many hadiths that state that he did it two times, but most of the Hadith describe that he did it three times. So washing our limbs one, two, or three times is correct, but anything more than that would be transgression.

The Prophet ﷺ was keen to warn his Companions against even this seemingly insignificant form of excess. Abdullah bin ʿAmr (may Allah be pleased with him) narrates that the Messenger of Allah ﷺ was passing by Saʿd (may Allah be pleased with him) when he was performing wudu'. He said, "What is this extravagance?" Saʿd said, "Messenger of Allah, can there be extravagance in wudu'?" The Messenger of Allah said: "Yes even if you're on the bank of a flowing river" (Ibn Majah—Daʿeef). This hadith is important to mention, even though it is weak, because it demonstrates a valuable point that is consistent with Islamic values.

We can see that even the most abundantly flowing rivers can dry up. This happened in multiple countries including America. There was a river called the Rio Grande (a Spanish name meaning "big river"). But it is now little more than a stream due to severe water withdrawal.

Caring about animals is also an Islamic value. Suraqah bin Juʿshum (may Allah be pleased with him) narrates: "I asked the Messenger of Allah ﷺ about a feral camel that comes to my water tank that I have prepared for my own camels: 'Will I be rewarded if I give it some water to drink?' He said: 'Yes, in every living being there is reward'" (Ibn Majah—Sahih).

Although in Islam, the dog is considered unclean and we are not to bring them inside our homes, Islam does not permit cruelty to dogs. Rather we know that it would displease Allah, and that caring for them brings immense reward.

Abu Huraira (may Allah be pleased with him) narrated that the Prophet ﷺ said, "A man felt very thirsty while he was travelling, and he came across a well. He went down the well, quenched his thirst and when he came out, he saw a dog panting and licking mud because of his excessive thirst. He said to himself, 'This dog is suffering from thirst as I did, so he went down the well again, filled his shoe with water, and let the dog drink. Allah thanked him for that deed and forgave him." The people said, "Allah's Messenger! Is there a reward for us in helping animals?" He replied, "Yes, there is a reward for helping any living being" (Bukhari, Abu Dawud, Muwatta Imam Malik, Adab Al Mufrad, Bulugh Al Maram—Sahih)

Abu Huraira (may Allah be pleased with him) also narrated that Allah's Messenger ﷺ said, "A prostitute was forgiven by Allah, because, passing by a panting dog near a well and seeing that the dog was about to die of thirst, she took off her shoe, tied it with her head-cover, and drew out some water for it. So Allah forgave her because of that" (Bukhari—Sahih).

Unfortunately humans have corrupted the earth. Allah the Exalted says:

ظَهَرَ ٱلْفَسَادُ فِى ٱلْبَرِّ وَٱلْبَحْرِ بِمَا كَسَبَتْ أَيْدِى ٱلنَّاسِ

Corruption has manifested in the land and in the sea because of the hands of men. (*Qur'an 30:41*)

It is our duty as Muslims to counter this trend. However there are many actions in our masjids that perpetuate the evil of extravagance rather than prevent it. In dinner parties or Iftar gatherings, the host often offers many types of food in the spirit of generosity. This, however, is a form of extravagance, and the guest feels an obligation to fill their plate beyond their capacity of consumption.

The average stomach of an adult male can't take more than twelve to sixteen ounces of food, and the size of our stomach is slightly larger than our fist. And so we often find much of the food discarded in the trash after events and dinners in the mosque. This is appalling considering most of us within living memory come from countries where hunger and poverty are widespread. Muslims are suffering from hunger in Gaza, Somalia, Eretria, Bangladesh, Myanmar, and Syria. This waste (referred to in the Qur'an as *isrāf*) is not permitted in Islam. Allah commands in the Qur'an:

وَءَاتِ ذَا ٱلْقُرْبَىٰ حَقَّهُۥ وَٱلْمِسْكِينَ وَٱبْنَ ٱلسَّبِيلِ وَلَا تُبَذِّرْ تَبْذِيرًا ﴿٢٦﴾ إِنَّ ٱلْمُبَذِّرِينَ كَانُوٓا۟ إِخْوَٰنَ ٱلشَّيَٰطِينِ وَكَانَ ٱلشَّيْطَٰنُ لِرَبِّهِۦ كَفُورًا ﴿٢٧﴾

And give the relative his right, and also the poor and the traveler, and do not spend wastefully. Indeed, the wasteful are brothers of the devils, and ever has Satan been to his Lord ungrateful. (*Qur'an 17:26-27*)

The host's intention of generosity causes him to offer a lot of food, but the guest should not take what he cannot finish. Allah describes to us:

وَٱلَّذِينَ إِذَآ أَنفَقُوا۟ لَمْ يُسْرِفُوا۟ وَلَمْ يَقْتُرُوا۟ وَكَانَ بَيْنَ ذَٰلِكَ قَوَامًا

And [they are] those who, when they spend, do so not excessively or sparingly but are ever, between that, [justly] moderate. (*Qur'an 25:67*)

Another common problem is the use of disposable water bottles. It is the duty of our masjids to pioneer ecologically and environmentally sound practices. This, after all is how our earlier generations understood Islam. Just one example for us to contemplate is how the architect Koca Mimar Sinan designed the Suleymaniye masjid in Turkey. One article details,

> Another factor he considered was the smoke that would come out from the 275 candles that would be used to light the prayer hall at night. He therefore designed the walls in such a way that the soot coming from the candles would be channeled into a special gallery inside the mosque, where it would be collected and later turned into a very fine ink. (. . .)
>
> In the 50s, when the Suleymaniye masjid was undergoing repairs, maintenance workers found a message written in Ottoman Turkish. After the message was transliterated and translated into modern Turkish, architects realized they had stumbled upon a personal message signed and dated by none other than the Sinan himself.
>
> The message read, 'As you have found this note, it means that one of the locking stones in the arch has slipped and you are unsure of how to replace it,' before going on to describe the necessary process required in doing so.[1]

1 World Bulletin News Desk. The Suleymaniye Mosque and the great architect Sinan. World Bulletin. 2014 (URL: https://www.worldbulletin.net/history/the-suleymaniye-mosque-and-the-great-architect-sinan-h127360.html)

Subḥān Allah! It is amazing how our earlier generations built masjids to last 500 years, contemplating the needs of the ummah for such long periods and designing them to survive and thrive in the environments in which they were built. This is our legacy and we should embrace it.

We make the following recommendations to promote environmental consciousness in the masjid:

- Install motion activated light switches.
- Install energy efficient LED light bulbs.
- Install energy efficient appliances (e.g., refrigerators, air conditioners).
- Install automatic thermostat controls to reduce energy usage.
- Install solar panels to capture electricity.
- Promote recycling.
- Ensure all disposable plates and cups are made from biodegradable materials.
- Restrict disposable water bottle usage.
- Establish a culture of minimizing food waste.
- Install water flow dampers in wuduʾ faucets.
- Install motion activated faucets in wuduʾ stations.

Chapter 10: Building the Masjid

Wherever Muslims resided over the centuries, we built masjids to meet our most fundamental religious need: to establish congregational prayer five times a day. But what should masjid architecture look like? A contemporary researcher explains:

> When Islam emerged in the seventh century, it didn't bring a specific architectural theory... What Islam brought was a set of values and themes, which could be applied differently depending on the environment in which the values are applied. This explains the wide variety of styles that had come out under the umbrella of Islamic Architecture... The philosophy of Islamic architecture is derived from the general philosophy of Islam ... Islamic philosophy focuses on the internal dynamics of the human entity in relationship with its external manifestations, integration between that entity and the Creator, and that the basic values of life are those related to the submission to the Creator, and equality among human beings... Islamic architecture is best articulated in its focus on the interior of the building, and the central arrangement of spaces ...
>
> If a building fulfilled these major elements, it could be described as a manifestation of Islamic architecture, regardless of the environment in which it was built. That is why; Islamic architecture took different forms depending on the environment in which it was applied. Islamic architecture in the desert was mainly different from its counterpart in tropical and polar areas. However, these forms share the major elements just outlined. One may also add that when the Muslims developed these concepts in different areas, they were influenced by local architectural prerequisites, tastes, and technical knowledge and expertise.[1]

All masjids have a common primary goal, which is to enable believers to connect with the Divine. Being a community center for the believers is its secondary purpose. The masjid also plays a central role as the primary gathering place for the Muslim community. It serves as a signifier for the presence of Muslims in the community. It also is a cultural site for the introduction of Islam to the non-Muslim community, connecting them to the rich histories of the Islamic civilization.

---

1 Abdelmonem, Mohamed; Selim, Gehan. Contemporary Islamic Architecture in the Arab World. 2003. https://www.researchgate.net/publication/320556990_Contemporary_Islamic_Architecture_in_the_Arab_World

Ideally, each masjid should have the following elements.

1. Entrance area & transition space
2. Prayer space (*Muṣallā*)
3. Wudu' station
4. Toilets
5. Shoe Rack
6. Pulpit (*mimbar*)
7. Prayer niche for the imam (*miḥrāb*)
8. Office for the imam & other administrators
9. Childcare area
10. Classrooms
11. Gymnasium
12. Meeting & event spaces
13. Minaret
14. Dome
15. External features (e.g., garden, courtyard, parking lot)
16. Social service areas (e.g., soup kitchen, heath clinic, orphanage)

We shall address each of these features in detail below. For illustrative purposes, we will discuss in this chapter the features needed in a masjid designed for a peak Jumuʿah attendance of 500 worshippers, and an Eid attendance of 1,000 worshippers.

Entrance Area

The entrance of the masjid is the first impression visitors have of the house of Allah. The masjid should provide a serene atmosphere to the worshiper through the functional and aesthetic use of the facility. The entrance area should be clean and neat, and remarkably beautiful; it should not be ugly or cluttered.

The entrance area needs to be separate from the *muṣallā*. The entrance of the masjid **cannot** be directly inside the muṣallā. When people enter the masjid, they track dirt, rain, and snow with their shoes. When people enter the masjid, they could be engaged in conversation with their friends, or continuing a conversation on their phones. The transition space enables people to change their behavior and frame of mind, and enter into a contemplative mood that is conducive to prayer.

The bathroom, wudu' station, and shoe rack **should not** be right at the entrance space. Entering a building and having to look at an open bathroom door or at a line of shoes is not the best greeting for our visitors. These spaces should be to one side, not directly in front of the main entrance.

Muṣallā

The *muṣallā* is the most important part of the masjid. The *muṣallā* should be clean. It should be carpeted and have padding beneath the carpet. The *muṣallā* should face the qiblah, and ideally it should not be at an angle that is not parallel to the room's walls.

وَمِنْ حَيْثُ خَرَجْتَ فَوَلِّ وَجْهَكَ شَطْرَ ٱلْمَسْجِدِ ٱلْحَرَامِ وَإِنَّهُۥ لَلْحَقُّ مِن رَّبِّكَ وَمَا ٱللَّهُ بِغَٰفِلٍ عَمَّا تَعْمَلُونَ

And wherever you go [for ṣalāh] turn your face toward the Masjid al-Haram, and indeed, it is the truth from your Lord. And Allah is not unaware of what you do. (*Qur'an 2:149*)

In the United States, for reasons of scarcity, it is common to see masjids that don't face the direction of prayer in their structure. In such cases, the lines of the prayer space must be laid at an angle to face the qibla.

The International Building Code for unconcentrated assembly is seven square feet per person. This is consistent with what we experience as masjid administrators. On average each person takes up seven square feet of space during ṣalāh. If the lines in the *muṣallā* are tilted at an angle, then on average it takes eight square feet per person because a lot of space is lost to the angles of the lines that don't match up with the direction of the walls. A masjid designed for a peak juma attendance of 500 worshippers will need 3,500 square feet of space in the *muṣallā* if the masjid faces the *qiblah,* and 4,000 square feet if the masjid is at an angle. When masjid designers try to squeeze additional lines into the same space, they make the space uncomfortable for those who are praying there.

In addition to this space designated for worshippers, designers should account for the space needed by the *miḥrāb*, the *mimbar,* and the closet for the sound and light systems—all of which could easily take up another 200-300 square feet. Walking through many masjids, it is obvious these issues were not considered until after the *muṣallā* had been built.

The *muṣallā* should have book shelves to hold copies of the Qur'an and other books often read by worshippers. The entry to the *muṣallā* should be from the back, not the sides and *definitely* not the front. It is best to position the *muṣallā* at the front and center of the masjid complex. The worshippers should enter from the back of the complex. The ancillary uses should ideally be positioned to the sides of the *muṣallā*.

Masjid administrators should invest in good acoustics for the *muṣallā*. Poor sound quality can seriously disrupt the prayer experience of those who come to worship. Hard surfaces cause echoes, especially if they are concrete walls parallel on opposite sides. The hardness of the walls can be reduced by installing sheetrock or wood paneling with design patterns on the surface to disrupt the echo effect. Another technique is to install sound clouds with various shapes and installed and varied angles. The sound clouds should be constructed from soft materials such as insulation foam, and can be carved or painted with classical Muslim designs. To this effect we also urge masjid administrators to invest in a professionally installed sound system, including an amplifier, a mixer, and wireless microphones and speakers.

There is a troubling trend among inexperienced masjid administrators of utilizing most of the masjid space for the *muṣallā*. In ideally constructed masjids, the *muṣallā* should take between twenty to thirty percent of the space of the masjid facility. Entryways, hallways, transition spaces, shoe and coat rooms, classrooms, offices, meeting spaces, banquet areas, and youth activity areas should take seventy to eighty percent of the space.

A masjid designed for a peak Jumuʿah attendance of 500 people should be between 15,000-20,000 square feet and should have a *muṣallā* that is 3,500-4,000 square feet. A masjid where the *muṣallā* takes up ninety percent of the space cannot provide the attendees sufficient bathrooms, wuduʾ stations, and places to keep their shoes and coats. A masjid where the *muṣallā* takes up eighty percent of the space cannot provide classrooms for the youth, who will then have to hold their classes in the *muṣallā*. A masjid where the *muṣallā* takes up fifty percent of the space cannot provide the worshippers a place to hold an Iftar dinner. In such masjids, the dinner must be held within the *muṣallā*, which can ruin the prayer carpet and leave the lingering smell of food. Any masjid where the muṣallā takes more than fifty percent of the space will significantly curtail the activities that can take place in that masjid.

Wuduʾ Station

Ideally the wuduʾ station should be separated from the toilets, located in a different location. The act of performing the wuduʾ should help the worshipper transition away from the hustle and bustle of daily life and prepare for a meeting with the Lord of the worlds.

In classical masjid designs, the wuduʾ station was typically beautified in the form of a lake, pond, or a water fountain. Sadly, in contemporary masjids, this is often the least attractive place in the entire facility. In modern constructions, a lot of masjids prefer to join the toilets and the wuduʾ station, primarily because of the significant cost impact of running plumbing to another location in the facility. The floor is constantly wet from the water runoff from the arms and feet of the worshippers, and that creates a slippery and dangerous environment. It also creates an odor problem.

Administrators scramble to mitigate these problems by placing heavy duty snow mats to prevent people from slipping on the floors and industrial fans on the ground to dry the floor. Neither of these enhance the beauty of the masjid. These problems can be better addressed with design solutions. For example, the entire floor of the wudu' station can be tilted, and water runoff drainage channels can be constructed. An air flow fan can also be installed within the walls of the wudu' station at the ground level to keep the floor dry at all times. The fan can be placed on an electric circuit with the lights to ensure the fan constantly runs when the wudu' station is occupied by people.

Another major problem is the amount of water flow in the wudu' stations. We recommend all masjids limit the volume of water flow by installing a damper inside each faucet. We also recommend motion sensors to control the length of time the water flows. Many motion sensor solutions have caused significant problems, however, so we recommend that masjid administrators survey the motion sensor systems in use at multiple masjids before they select their own solution.

The Messenger of Allah ﷺ used to perform wudu' with one *mudd* of water, and perform ghusl with just one ṣāʿ (Ibn Majah—Sahih). One *mudd* is defined as approximately 550 grams of water. We need to revive this sunnah. Most faucets in the wudu' stations are loose and frequently break. This usually happens as a result of people using the faucet to hold for balance as they perform the wudu'. For this problem, there are two solutions: install grab bars three inches above the faucets, and install a rivet on the wall connected to a harness firmly securing the faucet to the wall.

Toilets

The toilets should be separated from the wudu' station. There should also be a sufficient number of toilet stalls. Please check the relevant building code in the city where the masjid is located. Most building codes require a minimum number of toilet stalls based on the number of anticipated occupants. Despite whatever the building code permits, if the masjid does not have sufficient restroom availability, the worshippers will suffer. We recommend masjid administrators to exceed the minimum required number of toilet stalls by a factor of 30%. This will make the facility easier to use.

Additionally, the toilet stalls should be full privacy stalls. Most stalls have gaps in the hinges and the walls that violate Islamic norms of *hayā'* (modesty). The stall walls should extend to the floor and ceiling, or as close to them as possible. The toilets should have adequate exhaust fans and make up air units. The exhaust fan output should be vented through a different pipe from the sewer gas ventilation pipe. Not following this particular recommendation will cause the toilets to constantly emit an odor.

Shoe Rack

There must be no shoes on the floor in front of the shoe racks, endangering the safety of children and senior citizens. All shoes should be on shoe racks at all times. The shoe racks should not be in the immediate entry way. We recommend that a vestibule or side room be constructed for shoe racks and coat racks on one side of the entrance to the *muṣallā*.

Cubbies to hold shoes should exceed the number needed to ensure space for everyone, especially during peak attendance. The masjid administration should build (and store out of sight) extra shoe racks on wheels to be used at times of increased activity (such as Eid prayers). This will help prepare the masjid for accommodating large crowds without causing unsightly and unsafe messes.

Miḥrāb

The imam typically leads the ṣalāh from inside of a *miḥrāb*. This is the iconic niche at the front of every prayer hall indicating the direction of the prayer, as well as the imam's reserved position. The floor layout should provide clear visibility of the *miḥrāb* from the entrance, and all parts of the *muṣallā*, thus creating a focal point for attendees towards the *qiblah*.

In classical Islamic architecture, the *miḥrāb* was built as a semi-circular niche tapering to a concave top. It is often decorated like a giant doorway at the very center of the wall that faces the *qiblah*, almost as if it were a portal to the heavens. At the height of Muslim architecture, the *miḥrāb* was constructed to project the voice of the imam to the roof of the dome, which served as a reflecting surface to propagate the sound to the entire masjid. Current day miḥrābs should make proper arrangements for the microphone and sound system, so as to avoid feedback loops and echoes.

Mimbar (podium)

The *mimbar* is a raised platform from which sermons are delivered. The *mimbar* is located to the right of the *miḥrāb* on the qibla wall side of the masjid. It includes a short staircase leading to the top platform, where the speaker either sits or stands while addressing the congregation.

The Messenger of Allah ﷺ sent a person to a woman, asking her to instruct her carpenter to prepare a pulpit upon which he could address the people. The carpenter made a pulpit with three steps. Then the Messenger of Allah ﷺ commanded it to be placed where the current *mimbar* still stands. The hadith also mentions that it was fashioned out of the wood of al-Ghaba (Muslim—Sahih). Imam Ibn Rajab said: "The correct view is that the minbar had three steps, and it remained like that during the time of the Rightly Guided Caliphs." Imam Ibn Hajar Al Asqalani said: "The minbar remained as it was, with three steps, until it was increased to six steps by Marwaan during the caliphate of Muawiyah" (*Fath al-Baari* by Ibn Hajar, 2/399).

The *mimbar* of the Messenger of Allah ﷺ had three steps, but having more steps is not uncommon in masjids throughout the world. It is sometimes covered by a small dome. In some cases, a decorative gate or doorway may be placed at the bottom of the staircase, and it can also sometimes contain a bookcase. In some masjids, the *mimbar* is completely replaced by a simple podium or lectern. It is also sometimes replaced by an elaborate raised platform inside the *miḥrāb* to the right side of where the imam stands to lead ṣalāh.

Office for Imam and Administrators

A masjid fit to accomodate 500 worshippers should ideally have three offices. One can be used for the imam's day-to-day meetings and preparations, and two more for other administrational activities such related to finances, planning, and management. They can make do with fewer, but essential functions may be negatively impacted. Community members might be shy to speak to the imam about sensitive subjects if they do not feel that their meeting is private. It also ensures the safety of secure documents and information, especially those related to the masjid's finances.

Childcare Area

A dedicated daycare room should be provided if possible. If that's not possible, then at least a few toys for little children should be placed at the back of the *muṣallā* so that mothers can attend the masjid with their little children. It is not recommended to have toys that make noise or require batteries. Many larger masjids also have a separate "mother and baby" *muṣallā* and a separate "father and baby" *muṣallā*, where parents with little children can join the prayer without disrupting the rest of the masjid.

Classrooms

A masjid built for a peak Jumuʿah audience of 500 should have between six and twelve classrooms.

Gymnasium

Including a gymnasium in the masjid compound is a very novel idea, as there are no classical masjids found with anything of the sort. This may be because those societies engaged their youth in other ways. Nowadays, especially in the United States, it has become imperative for the masjid to have youth recreation areas. Unless we as a Muslim community make urgent investments in our youth, we are at risk of losing the next generation of Muslims.

Ideally the gym should be the same size as the *muṣallā*. It should be placed behind the *muṣallā* (from the direction of the *qiblah*) so that the gym can also be used as overflow for Eid and other large prayers. For basketball purposes, the gym should be 25 feet high, but a height of 20 feet can be sufficient in many cases. It should have appropriate gym flooring with bounce/cushioning to protect the knees of the youth after long term use. The gym should also install impact padding on the walls to minimize the risk of injury. The ceiling lights and the light switches in the gym should be installed within protective cages to protect them from being damaged by any sports equipment.

Meeting Spaces

The masjid needs multiple meeting spaces, including at least one large meeting space which can be used as a banquet hall. One space should also provide soft seating so people can have small group meetings and discussions.

Minaret

The minaret is a distinctive feature of Islamic architecture. It originally served as the place from where the call to prayer was made. In classical designs, it is typically surrounded by one or more projecting galleries from where the muezzin announces the adhan (call to prayer). In most modern masjids in Muslim countries, the adhan is called from the *muṣallā* by microphone to a speaker system installed on the minaret.

It may be argued that the minaret's purpose today is more symbolic. It serves as a visual reminder of the Muslim presence in a city. Over the centuries, it has become the most distinctive piece of Muslim architecture.

Scholars agree that al-Masjid al-Nabawi did not have a minaret during the life of the Messenger of Allah ﷺ. There is historical debate about the first minaret. Some scholars have described a minaret during the reign of Caliph Walid bin Abdul-Malik in 72 AH/691 CE. By the end of the Umayyad period, minarets were common, and they are now an established part of the cultural heritage of the Islamic civilization.

If constructed in an American context, the primary purpose of the minaret would be to serve as an aesthetic indication of the Muslim presence, marking the diversity and inclusion of a community. As such, it should be visually distinct from a church steeple. If a masjid chooses to install a minaret, it should be sturdy and slender. The minaret should be lighted at night to highlight its role as ambassador for Islam.

Dome (Qubba)

The green dome of al-Masjid al-Nabawi is instantly recognizable to every Muslim across the world today. However, its original structure did not have a dome. It is interesting to consider, then why many masjids nowadays are decorated with a dome on the roof.

This architectural element initially held no spiritual or symbolic significance and was purely functional. From a structural engineering perspective, a dome can be thought of as an arch spun on its y-axis. The main function of an arch is to increase the distance that can be spanned without placing an additional pillar using the same construction materials. Explained in very simple terms, placing arches or domes under the roof allows a building of equal size to be constructed using fewer pillars. The dome exerts thrusts all around its perimeter, unlike the regular arch, which exerts thrust upon only two pillars or walls. So originally, the dome was constructed (by Muslims and people of other faiths alike) for structural engineering purposes to create large spaces while minimizing pillars within them. Over time this unique structure became a declaration of a building's majesty and grandeur. As such temples, churches, masjids, legislatures, and many other places of assembly are frequently adorned with a dome.

Domes were flaunted all throughout history by any society who wished to express its power and authority through architecture. One researcher writes,

> The symbol of the Dome of Rock became a symbol of centrality, authority and power. Rome, the capital of one of the most powerful empires in history, is symbolized by a dome, namely the Pantheon. In many modern day world capitals, the first image that comes to

> one's mind is that of a beautiful structure with a dome. Just to name a few St. Basil's church in Russia, St. Paul's Cathedral in London, the United States Capitol building, and the Millennium Dome in London.[2]

The first dome built by the Muslims is widely considered to be the Dome of the Rock (*Qubbat al-Ṣakhrah*) in Jerusalem. Its construction was completed by the Caliph Abdul-Malik bin Marwan in 71 AH / 691 CE.[3] Soon thereafter, the symbol was adopted by mosques all around.[4]

Still, a dome is not essential for any masjid. And many masjids constructed in modern times have chosen to skip constructing a dome. We urge masjid administrators to seek the help of a structural engineer with experience designing domes before making any decisions about installing a dome in the masjid.

External Features

In traditional masjids, it is common to have a large central courtyard (ṣaḥn), which is surrounded by an arcade (*riwāq*) on all sides. Traditional masjid courtyards contain a public water fountain basin (*ḥawḍ*), where worshippers perform wudu' before ṣalāh. But despite how common it may be among classical style masjids, a courtyard is not a religiously mandated architectural feature. It developed over time to provide free flowing air movement into the masjid, improve aesthetic beauty, and serve as overflow worship space for large Eid or Jumuʿah gatherings. Many masjids, especially since the twentieth century, do not have a courtyard. Even though the need for overflow prayer space is met with the construction of a gymnasium, and the wudu' stations are usually placed inside of the building, we still strongly urge all masjids to have landscaping, flower gardens, or other forms of natural beauty outside the masjid. Another vital feature of modern masjids is access to mass transit or parking. Masjids need adequate parking. A masjid designed for 500 Juma attendees should have a minimum of 150 parking spots. Masjid administrators should also take into account access to mass transit. To neglect making the masjid accessible to commuters and those who do not live close enough to walk to the masjid will severely diminish the masjid's impact on its community.

2 Mahnaz Shujrah. Domes in Islamic Architecture: Understanding their Symbolism and Evolution Overtime. Timsaal. Reflections on Society and Culture. September 23, 2018. (URL: https://www.timsaal.com/domes-in-islamic-architecture-understanding-their-symbolism-and-evolution-overtime/)

3 Stephen Langfur. Dome of the Rock. Near East Tourist Agency. (URL: http://www.netours.com/content/view/160/26/)

4 Robert Hillenbrand. The Mosque in the Medieval Islamic World. Islamic Arts and Architecture. October 7, 2011 (URL: http://islamic-arts.org/2011/the-mosque-in-the-medieval-islamic-world/)

Social Service Areas

The masjid should have designated space for social services. The basic minimum social service a masjid can provide is a food pantry. A separate food storage space should be provided. Other ideas for social services that require relatively small spaces are tutoring programs and free medical clinics (outpatient). In classical times, the standard masjid complex included soup kitchens and orphanages.

Masjid Security

The security of the worshippers at the masjid should be a major concern for the administrators. We make the following specific security recommendations:

- Periodically analyze the design and layout of the masjid for potential security threats.
- Ensure entrances and exits are sufficiently wide to allow for rapid egress during emergencies.
- Install door and window locks, barred entryways, fencing, and gate locks as needed.
- Install a security camera system. Ensure every wall and angle of the masjid is covered with a security camera. (Note: in some masjids, privacy concerns might prevent the installation of cameras inside of the masjid.)
- Ensure the security camera system automatically updates to the cloud to assure access if the recorders are stolen or destroyed.
- Develop notification protocol specifying who should be contacted in emergencies.
- Install safety lighting around the perimeter of the entire masjid activated by motion sensors.
- Install adequate lighting in the parking lot.
- Buffer parking lot from the masjid building with green space.
- Erase graffiti on the same day it appears after taking pictures of it.
- Install a burglar alarm system.
- Strategically landscape the property by cutting down hedges or bushes where intruders can conceal themselves.
- Form a security committee to patrol the premises, especially during high attendance.
- Contact local police and arrange for more security patrols of the areas surrounding the masjid.
- Record all hate messages or harassment in a security journal.

- Report all hate messages or harassment to Law Enforcement.
- Develop and implement a security plan for computer and information systems hardware and software, including a firewall, recovery and restoration plans to return computer systems to full functionality after an incident.
- In cold weather states, install frozen pipe sensors to alert management of severe temperature drops in pipes before the pipes burst and cause major damage.
- In cold weather states, install boiler temperature sensors to alert management of unexpected boiler shutdowns before any major damage.

Masjid Facility Budget Issues

Any facility, including masjid facilities, need to make periodic capital improvements. For example: the roof needs to be replaced every 25 years, the air conditioner units need to be replaced every 15 years, the parking lot needs to be repaved every 15 years, and most heavy duty boiler plants need to be replaced every 40 years. Every masjid should annually set-aside a "Capital Improvements Reserve Fund" for these easily predictable maintenance projects.

The amount that should be placed every year into the "Capital Improvements Reserve Fund" should be $1.50 per square foot per year (though it should be higher for older buildings). So the administrators of a 10,000 square foot masjid building should set aside $15,000 per year for capital improvement. In some years, the fund will have a very large surplus; it is very important to make sure that the masjid does not spend this money on operating expenses. Those funds can be used for other improvements that must be made throughout the years.

The masjid facility needs constant repairs and maintenance in addition to these capital improvements. These are the types of repairs that are done every month, such as light fixtures, plumbing fixtures, damaged carpets ,and broken tiles that need to be replaced. We recommend every masjid to have a budget item of $1.50 to $2.00 per square foot per year in repairs and maintenance costs. Some masjids go into emergency mode whenever they need routine repairs or periodic capital improvements. This is a sign of poor planning. Masjid administrators need to be proactive in planning for the upkeep and maintenance of their masjid. A respected architect with experience designing many masjids pointed out to me that masjids are grotesquely underfunded for construction projects, and that renovation and repair costs for masjids can run much higher than the estimates above!

Masjid leadership should limit access to the capital funds. Many masjids have a tendency to dip into restricted capital funds to cover operating expenses. They then either neglect or are unable to replenish those funds. This will create undue hardship when the funds are needed. It is best to isolate such funds, limit access to them and invest them in a secure liquid investment. Two of the waqf organizations listed later in this book conveniently provide this service to masjids.

Establishing a New Masjid Facility

When establishing a new masjid, administrators must make the choice between building a new structure or renovating an existing facility. In many cases, refurbishing an existing building is cheaper. But if masjid administrators were unable to plan correctly, renovation could be more expensive than new construction in the long run, after the Total Cost of Ownership (TCO) is considered. We strongly urge masjid administrators to consult professionals to ensure the longevity and sustainability of their organizations.

In 2020, the average cost of new construction of a commercial building, excluding the cost of acquiring land, ranged from $200-300 per square foot depending upon the installed features. Existing facilities such as retail stores, existing churches, or old school buildings may be available for purchase for prices ranging from $50-$75 per square foot. The renovation costs range from $20-$80 per square foot depending upon the installed features. A new construction of a 20,000 square foot masjid could cost between $4 million to $6 million. An existing 20,000 square foot facility refurbished as a masjid might cost between $1.4 million to $3.1 million.

The following factors should be considered when renovating an existing facility as a masjid:

- Thorough inspections should be performed prior to purchase.
- The space can be used as a masjid sooner.
- Less costs necessary before masjid space can be used.
- It is easier to fundraise for a project that is already delivering services to the community.
- Total cost of ownership (TCO) is often lower.
- Frequently the architectural plans and "as-built" drawings are not available for existing facilities. This leads to expensive surprises during construction such as plumbing, electrical and HVAC issues.
- Once renovation begins, you will probably be required to bring the entire facility up to the current code.
- Asbestos used in buildings erected before the 1980s is a major issue.

- Less efficient layout may entail a lot of wasted space.
- Older buildings are usually less energy efficient.

The following factors should be considered when building a new masjid:

- Everything is designed for use as a masjid.
- Less maintenance is required for the first two decades of ownership.
- New building technology is more energy efficient.
- Efficient layout will minimize wasted space.
- There will be a long delay before the property can be first used as a masjid.
- More costs will be involved before the property can be used as a masjid.
- Price estimates are less accurate in new construction projects.
- Planners should always expect and plan for costs overruns.

Building Code Compliance

Many masjid administrators are ignorant or negligent of the importance of complying with building codes. This is troubling, as the main purpose of the building code is to protect the health, safety, and welfare of the public regarding the construction and occupancy of buildings. This means that, in the case of a masjid, the building code exists to protect the worshippers inside.

For example, we have heard masjid administrators complaining about being "forced" to install sprinklers, fire-rated doors, and panic bars. These features would save the lives of Muslim worshippers in case of a fire or terrorist attack on the masjid! Why would a masjid administrator resist these regulations? Would any of us want to be responsible for the deaths of worshippers in our masjid?

Masjid administrators also often think of the building code regulations as a maximum. Many times there are no extra measures taken in caution. We encourage masjid administrators to think of them instead as a safety minimum, and to construct features that will serve their worshippers better, even if they are not required by the building codes.

Chapter 11: Beautifying the Masjid

The human soul is naturally attracted to beauty and art. Beauty and elegance are Islamic values. The Messenger of Allah ﷺ said: “Allah is beautiful and loves beauty” (Bukhari—Sahih). Allah the Exalted says,

قُلْ مَنْ حَرَّمَ زِينَةَ ٱللَّهِ ٱلَّتِىٓ أَخْرَجَ لِعِبَادِهِۦ وَٱلطَّيِّبَٰتِ مِنَ ٱلرِّزْقِ

“Say, who has forbidden the beauty which Allah has brought forth for his servants, and the good things of sustenance” (*Qur’an 7:32*)

Our Lord further emphasized this concept:

يَٰٓأَيُّهَا ٱلَّذِينَ ءَامَنُوا۟ لَا تُحَرِّمُوا۟ طَيِّبَٰتِ مَآ أَحَلَّ ٱللَّهُ لَكُمْ وَلَا تَعْتَدُوٓا۟ إِنَّ ٱللَّهَ لَا يُحِبُّ ٱلْمُعْتَدِينَ

“O believers, do not prohibit the good things which Allah has made lawful to you and do not transgress. Indeed, Allah does not like transgressors.” (*Qur’an 5:87*)

The Ambassador of Islamic Civilization

Art is more than aesthetics; it has served for centuries as a powerful ambassador for the theology and values of Islam. A professor of religious studies explains:

> Masterpieces of Islamic civilization communicate the beauty and truth of its revelation with a profound directness simply unmatched by articles or books about Islam... despite the dissemination of virulent propaganda against Islam in the West, many people from Western societies queue for hours to admire the architecture of the Alhambra in Spain and the Taj Mahal in India as well as exhibitions of Islamic calligraphy and miniature paintings
>
> The true source of Islamic art is the Islamic revelation, not its historical precedents or influences. This singular origin accounts for its remarkable unity across time and space... The Islamic arts also all bear the imprint of the Qur’an.[1]

1 Oludamini Ogunnaike. The Silent Theology of Islamic Art. Renovatio, The Journal Of Zaytuna College. Dec 5, 2017 (URL: https://renovatio.zaytuna.edu/article/the-silent-theology-of-islamic-art)

Islamic Calligraphy

Islam absolutely prohibits depicting images of God. This prohibition paved the way for a more subtle calligraphy. This is also because reading, writing and the pen are highly emphasized in Islam.

ٱقْرَأْ وَرَبُّكَ ٱلْأَكْرَمُ ﴿٣﴾ ٱلَّذِى عَلَّمَ بِٱلْقَلَمِ ﴿٤﴾ عَلَّمَ ٱلْإِنسَٰنَ مَا لَمْ يَعْلَمْ ﴿٥﴾

"Read! And your Lord is most Generous. He taught by the pen. Taught humanity what they didn't know." (*Qur'an 96:3-5*)

The Messenger of Allah ﷺ said: "Whoever recites a letter from the book of Allah will receive the reward for it, and ten times as much" (Tirmidhi–Hassan). Islamic calligraphy is not merely about decoration and beauty, rather it is primarily a means to connect human beings to Allah. The uniqueness of Islamic calligraphy is well established among western historians. One describes,

> The development of sophisticated calligraphy as an art form is not unique to Islamic culture. Other examples include Chinese and Japanese calligraphy and illuminated bibles... In the Islamic world, however, calligraphy has been used to a much greater extent and in astonishingly varied and imaginative ways, which have taken the written word far beyond pen and paper into all art forms and materials. For these reasons, calligraphy may be counted as a uniquely original feature of Islamic art. The genius of Islamic calligraphy lies not only in the endless creativity and versatility, but also in the balance struck by calligraphers between transmitting a text and expressing its meaning through a formal aesthetic code.[2]

The ultimate goal of Islamic calligraphy is for the worshipper to be overwhelmed by the words of Allah as described in this verse,

إِذَا تُتْلَىٰ عَلَيْهِمْ ءَايَٰتُ ٱلرَّحْمَٰنِ خَرُّوا سُجَّدًا وَبُكِيًّا

"When the verses of the Most Merciful are recited to them, they fall down prostrate in adoration and tears." (*Qur'an 19:58*)

2 Calligraphy in Islamic Art. Victoria and Albert Museum. (URL: http://www.vam.ac.uk/content/articles/c/calligraphy-in-islamic-art/)

Geometric Patterns

Geometry constitutes the second major category of Islamic art. Muslim artists developed the craft of creating patterns and shapes as a substitute for images of humans and animals. They utilized a wide variety of intricate and complex patterns by repeated combinations of squares, circles, and triangles.

Geometric patterns occur in a variety of Islamic art including woodwork, stone carvings, stained glass, metalwork, tilework, decorative vaulting, screens, ceramics, leather, carpeting, and woven textiles. Abstract geometric art is particularly favored in masjids because it encourages spiritual reflection. Their patterns are designed to spark contemplation of the underlying reality, rather than merely being a decoration.

Under no circumstances are images of people or animals allowed in masjid artwork. We have seen unfortunate cases where miniature pictures of crosses or Hindu deities were found on the prayer carpet. Often this happens when carpets are purchased from non-Muslim manufacturers who do not understand the requirements of art in the Islamic context.

Perfumes

The use of perfumes is another sunnah relevant to the masjid. Aisha narrates that the Messenger of Allah ﷺ "commanded us to build masjids in different localities and that they should be kept clean and be perfumed" (Abu Dawud, Tirmidhi, Ibn Majah—Sahih).

We are especially encouraged to use perfume when attending large gatherings. The Messenger of Allah ﷺ informed us of the etiquette of going to Jumuʿah prayer with many people. He said: "It is a duty for the Muslims to bathe on Friday, and to wear some perfume. If he does not find any, then water is a perfume for him" (Tirmidhi—Sahih).

When going to hajj, he ﷺ also applied perfume. Aishah said: "I used to put perfume on the Messenger of Allah ﷺ using the best perfume I could find, until I saw the perfume glistening on his head and in his beard, before he entered Ihram" (Nasa'i—Sahih). He appreciated good perfume even outside of the masjid. Ibn Abbas said, "I saw the Messenger of Allah ﷺ perfume his head with musk" (Ibn Majah—Sahih). Anas (may Allah be pleased with him) said, "Indeed the Prophet ﷺ would not refuse perfume" (Bukhari, Tirmidhi—Sahih). The Messenger of Allah ﷺ also specified, "The best of perfume is musk" (Nasa'i—Sahih).

Fiqh of masjid Decoration

The Messenger of Allah ﷺ discouraged the construction of excessively fancy and luxurious facilities for the masjids. He ﷺ said: "I was not commanded to build high masjids" (Abu Dawud—Sahih). He ﷺ also warned us that competing in constructing masjids as a monument to one's vanity is one of the signs of the Day of Judgment. He ﷺ said, "The Last Hour will not come until people compete with one another in building masjids" (Abu Dawud, Ibn Majah—Sahih).

In an attempt to translate all the values mentioned in this chapter into the masjid experience, we make the following recommendations:

- The masjid should not have excessive decorations that serve no purpose in Islam.
- The masjid should be perfumed.
- The application of the perfume should not be excessive because many worshippers suffer from asthma and other problems.
- The masjid should be adorned with Islamic art and calligraphy for the purpose of reminding worshippers of Allah.
- There is no harm in having geometric art to create a contemplative atmosphere for worshippers to enter into a contemplative mood.
- The use of artwork should not be excessive nor should it distract the worshipper from the ṣalāh.
- Any artwork in the masjid should not contain images of people or animals.
- Administrators should ensure the carpet of the muṣallā does not contain any pictures.

Chapter 12: Protecting the Masjid

The first *waqf* established in this Ummah was the masjid of Quba. The Messenger of Allah ﷺ personally placed its first stones as soon as he arrived there on his way to Medina, laying the foundations for the first property to be entrusted for public use. The linguistic meaning of the word *waqf* (pl. *awqāf*) comes from the root word *wa-qa-fa*, meaning "to stop, prevent or restrain".

The idea of a *waqf* is not a modern invention. It actually came from the Messenger of Allah ﷺ upon laying the foundations for the masjid of Quba. He also advised Umar bin al-Khattab to donate his land in Khaybar as a *waqf* for poor people.

When the Muslims first arrived in Medina, it had a severe shortage of water. The well of Rūmah was the only source of drinkable water for many people. Taking advantage of this situation, the owner of the well charged very high prices for water, so the Messenger of Allah ﷺ promised forgiveness and reward to whoever would buy it and dedicate it for the Muslim Ummah. Uthman bin ʿAffan (may Allah be pleased with him) purchased it immediately and donated it as a *waqf*.

Interestingly enough, this *waqf* of Uthman (may Allah be pleased with him) continues to exist today even after fourteen centuries. It generates income, manages investments, and gives charity on behalf of its founder. May Allah be pleased with him and increase his honor.[1]

Abdullah bin Umar (may Allah be pleased with him) narrates that in the lifetime of the Messenger of Allah ﷺ, Umar (may Allah be pleased with him) gave in charity some of his property, a garden of date-palms at Thamagh. Umar said, "Messenger of Allah, I have some property that I love dearly and I want to give it away in charity." The Messenger of Allah ﷺ said: "Give it as an endowment with its land and trees on the condition that the land and trees will neither be sold, nor given as a present, nor bequeathed; the fruits are to be spent in charity" (Sahih—al-Bukhari).

The actual charter of Umar bin al-Khattab's *waqf* read as follows:

> In the name of Allah, the Compassionate, the Merciful. This is what the servant of Allah, Umar, Commander of the Faithful, directs upon his death. The land at Thamagh, its servant Sirma bin Akwa who re-

1 SPA Madina. After 1,400 years, water still flows in Uthman ibn Affan well in Madina. Al Arabiya. 2018 (URL: https://english.alarabiya.net/en/life-style/travel-and-tourism/2018/03/11/After-1400-years-water-still-flows-in-Uthman-ibn-Affan-well-in-Madina.html)

> sides there, the hundred shares of land in the valley of Khaibr which Muhammad ﷺ granted to me will remain in the custody of Hafsah during her life, then the leaders of her family will be in charge of these endowments. These will neither be sold nor purchased, spending its produce among the poor as directed by the custodian. The custodian is permitted a salary and to retain assistants. (Abu Dawud)

This hadith gives us an explicit understanding of the *waqf* contract. After the battle of Khaybar, a lot of lands came to the Messenger of Allah ﷺ. He divided them between the companions. Umar bin al-Khattab (may Allah be pleased with him) was granted a piece of land there. He used to love this land dearly because the Messenger of Allah ﷺ personally gave it to him. Therefore he gave the best of what he loved. The Messenger of Allah ﷺ commanded him not to give it as a one-time *sadaqah* but to make it a *waqf.* Through it we understand the concept of how the *waqf* was first implemented in the first generation.

One value of *waqf* for someone like Uthman or Umar (may Allah be pleased with them) is the concept of continuous charity. Giving charity to somebody yields a reward for one deed. But setting up a resource for continuous benefit for generations to come would be a means of extending one's return on investment.

The concept of *waqf* in Fiqh is to take an asset and restrict its use forever to charitable purposes. The technical legal term used for the original body of the *waqf* is "corpus." So if a person has a farm of a hundred acres as *waqf,* that hundred acres of land is considered the corpus, and the revenue that comes from it is called the usufruct, which is the dedicated revenue that is sent every year to the charitable purpose (such as supporting a masjid).

In most Muslim countries, the *waqf* is an automatic provision of the law. When a donor establishes a masjid on any piece of land in most Muslim countries, a legal provision immediately takes over. After the donor dies, his children and heirs do not have the power to sell the land, because the law does not allow this.

This, however, is not the case in America. Under the American legal system masjids (which generally follow the rulings of churches) are corporations.

> The result of the legislature's reform was a 1784 Act to enable all the religious Denominations in this State to appoint Trustees, who shall be a Body Corporate ... The Act then laid out the procedures by which any "church, congregation, or religious society" could gain incorporation" ... In case after case, unincorporated churches – which

either found themselves in jurisdictions that did not statutorily authorize incorporation or which had simply failed to avail themselves of such statutes – were transformed into corporations by the courts as a necessary requirement of equity.[2]

Under American law, pieces of land are owned by people or corporations, and corporations are controlled by their boards. In general, the board that has the right to buy a piece of land also has the right to sell it.

Under American law, there is nothing legally called a *waqf*. Available legal instruments include the irrevocable charitable trust or a land conservation agreement or charitable foundation. These perform some functions that normally in Islamic society a *waqf* would perform. They also differ significantly from the *waqf* in many ways.

Consider if a masjid were built, then all the founders of that masjid died, and various people from the neighborhood became board members. Decades later, the new board of the masjid could decide to use the space for non-Islamic purposes. Under American law, if the board decides to do so, then no legal action can be taken to stop them unless some precautionary restriction exists, such as a waqf contract. Compare this lack of structure to the powerful and specific language in the charter written by Umar (may Allah be pleased with him). The *waqf* system is meant to prevent this distortion of purpose for the masjid. It is like fire insurance: unappreciated until there is a fire.

In America, a masjid or a church in many respects, is a corporation like any other corporation. Its assets are subject to seizure and forfeiture. Since 1984 various Catholic dioceses and religious orders have paid out almost $3 billion in court-imposed judgments and out of court settlements, and 19 dioceses of the Catholic Church have filed for bankruptcy for various acts of sexual abuse committed by Catholic clergy. In these cases many churches and other properties have been sold off to pay for the costs of litigation defense and to pay the court imposed judgments and out of court settlements.[3]

Similar to the case mentioned above, if the non-profit corporation owning the real estate of the masjid is sued and loses, the law will force the non-profit corporation to sell the masjid to satisfy the outstanding judgment. A

2 Kellen Funk. Church Corporations And The Conflict Of Laws In Antebellum America. Journal of Law and Religion. 32 No 2. 2017 (URL: https://www.cambridge.org/core/journals/journal-of-law-and-religion/article/church-corporations-and-the-conflict-of-laws-in-antebellum-america/143A81DC7AAA8A6FFE90E6F8BB424893/core-reader)

3 NCR Staff. Catholic dioceses and orders that filed for bankruptcy and other major settlements. National Catholic Reporter. 2018 (URL: https://www.ncronline.org/news/accountability/catholic-dioceses-and-orders-filed-bankruptcy-and-other-major-settlements)

wrongful death lawsuit arising from a drowning death in a summer camp can generate a court judgment exceeding $5,000,000. An injury related to a slip in the parking lot can generate a court judgment exceeding $300,000.

In Europe and India, many masjids that were constructed with the utmost beauty and grandeur under the Muslims who used to rule the land are no longer allowed to function as masjids. The most regrettable examples are the Alhambra in Spain and one of the two masjids next to Taj Mahal, where Muslims are no longer allowed to pray in. This is because the Muslim rulers who built those masjids relied upon the standard legal system of the Muslim country to protect the masjid. Thus when the country was no longer ruled by a Muslim king, the masjid was no longer protected. This is true in the lands ruled in the past by Muslim rulers but ruled today by non-Muslim systems. These include Spain, Portugal, Bulgaria, Romania, Czech Republic, Serbia, Croatia, and India. It also includes the Chechnya & Dagestan republics of Russia, the Xinjiang, Gansu & Ningxia provinces of China, the Arakan state of Myanmar, the Pattani & Yala provinces of Thailand, and the Mindanao region of the Philippines. In all these lands, because the masjids relied upon the standard Islamic legal system, without establishing a separate *waqf*, the status of any particular masjid can be jeopardized.

Salahuddin al-Ayyubi, may Allah be pleased with him, liberated Jerusalem and Masjid al-Aqsa, the third holiest site in Islam, from the crusaders, who had prevented Muslims from praying there for many decades. However the crusaders continued occupying large sections of Palestine even after his victory. He feared they might reverse his victory and prevent people from worshipping there, so he set up a *waqf*. This is not customary for a Muslim ruler because they typically relied upon the Islamic legal system of the country to safeguard *waqfs*.

Due to the precarious circumstances, he set up a separate *waqf* in the year 531 AH/1137 CE. This *waqf* was subsequently modified several times in Muslim history. The effectiveness of his legal arrangements were not fully tested for another 830 years, in 1387 AH/1967 CE when the Muslims lost Jerusalem again. A researcher explains:

> With regard to the waqf in Palestine, the truly important turning point was the start of the British Mandate... With the exception of brief periods of Crusader rule between 1099 and 1187, Palestine had been governed by Muslims for 1,300 years... The Muslim code of law - the sharia - applied to Muslims, who thought of themselves as the umma (nation). Non-Muslims had the status of belonging to a recognized religious community (taifa) under the millet system. The British occupation of Palestine was now ruled by a non-Muslim

government, and the Muslims ceased to be the "nation". They, in turn, now had the status of a religious community - one of several.[4]

The existence of this *waqf* is the number one reason why masjid al-Aqsa remains in Muslim hands today. May Allah honor Salahuddin al-Ayyubi for his wisdom and his service to Islam.

Allah the Exalted commands:

إِنَّ ٱللَّهَ يَأْمُرُكُمْ أَن تُؤَدُّوا ٱلْأَمَـٰنَـٰتِ إِلَىٰٓ أَهْلِهَا

"Indeed Allah commands you to render back trusts to their owners." (*Qur'an 4: 58*)

As we know, Allah is the owner of the masjid, so masjid administrators have an affirmative duty to ensure the masjid remains dedicated to the pleasure of Allah. Furthermore, Allah praises the believers who fulfil their trusts:

وَٱلَّذِينَ هُمْ لِأَمَـٰنَـٰتِهِمْ وَعَهْدِهِمْ رَٰعُونَ

"And those who honor their trusts and their contracts." (*Qur'an 23:8*)

Therefore we strongly urge masjid administrators to secure every masjid in a *waqf*. The benefits of the *waqf* are:

1. Maintain the Sunnah of our noble Prophet Muhammad ﷺ and following in the footsteps of his companions, may Allah be pleased with them.
2. Shield real estate from the ability of a future board to sell it.
3. Shield real estate from the ability of a future board to convert it to an un-Islamic purpose.
4. Shield institutional real estate from potential legal liabilities and court judgments.
5. Shield institutional real estate from becoming the target of a board takeover attempt.
6. Provide a vehicle for ongoing sadaqah from profits of a business.
7. Receive technical assistance from the *waqf* organization.

In America, there are three main *waqf* organizations in the Sunni community. The Shia community has several other *waqfs*.

North American Islamic Trust (NAIT)

NAIT stands for North American Islamic Trust. It is the first and largest American waqf organization. It was incorporated in Indiana in 1393

4 Reiter, Yitzhak (1996). Islamic Endowments in Jerusalem Under British Mandate. Routledge. ISBN 0714643424. (URL: https://books.google.com/books?id=SJOaAgAAQBAJ)

AH/1973 CE. It has a 501(c)(3) status approved by the IRS. It has approximately 4000 properties in the waqf program with over a billion dollars in assets. It also operates the Iman Mutual Funds, American Trust Publications, and the Islamic Centers Cooperative Fund, a unique and safe investment vehicle available exclusively for Islamic organizations.

Islamophobes have attacked NAIT viciously and relentlessly for many years now. In 1428 AH/2007 CE, at the repeated insistence of notorious Islamophobes, the U.S. Department of Justice listed NAIT as an unindicted co-conspirator in a terrorism trial. After repeated unsuccessful attempts to get them to correct this egregious error, NAIT sued the U.S. Department of Justice and in a testament to their organizational prowess, NAIT won.

After NAIT won, the U.S. Department of Justice appealed this ruling and lost. In 1431 AH/2010 CE the Fifth Circuit Court of Appeals found that the U.S. Department of Justice violated the Fifth Amendment rights of NAIT by naming them in public as unindicted co-conspirators in 1428 AH/2007 CE. The court called it "simply an untested allegation of the government made in anticipation of a possible evidentiary dispute that never came to pass." Both the Bush and Obama administrations declined to initiate any new prosecutions after consideration of the facts.

Muslim American Waqf Incorporated (MAWI)

MAWI stands for Muslim American Waqf Incorporated. It was originally started as Muslim Endowment and Community Asset Foundation (MECA) in North Carolina in 1431 AH/2010 CE. It has a 501(c)(2) status approved by the IRS. The trust held only a few properties. However in 1440AH/2019 CE they reincorporated in Delaware and acquired 501(c)(3) status from the IRS.

Minnesota Education Trust (MET)

The Minnesota Education Trust (MET), also called the Minnesota Waqf, was incorporated in Minnesota in 1428 AH/2007 CE, it has 501(c)(3) status approved by the IRS. It holds less than two dozen properties and operates 8 Endowments and Donor Advised Funds. In 1432 AH/2011 CE, despite a three year, 5 million dollar federal litigation, plaintiffs failed to breach the Waqf contract for two of the facilities to liquidate them.

To our knowledge, there are only these three waqf organizations in America run by Sunni organizations. We encourage all masjid administrators to uphold their responsibilities to the masjid by placing it in a *waqf*.

Chapter 13: Legal & Organizational Issues

In addition to being the house of Allah, the masjid is also a nonprofit organization. The rules of proper nonprofit management also apply to operating and managing a masjid. Allah the Exalted commands us to be organized:

يَـٰٓأَيُّهَـا ٱلَّذِيـنَ ءَامَنُـوا خُـذُوا حِذْرَكُـمْ فَٱنفِـرُوا ثُبَـاتٍ أَوِ ٱنفِـرُوا جَمِيعًـا

"O believers, take your precautions and proceed in groups or proceed all together." (*Qur'an 4:71*)

Masjid Boards

Many masjid boards make the mistake of not meeting for very long periods of time. This unfortunately leads to poor management. One way to have useful board meetings is to establish an annual board work plan. Each of the items of the board work plan should be performed in one or more separate meetings.

The board work plan should include approving the annual budget; approving the annual board work plan; reviewing the annual financial statements, including the 990 and audit (if applicable); electing directors and officers; a performance review of Executive Director and other senior leadership; and developing and updating the strategic plan.

Every masjid should perform a SWOT analysis, or one of the available alternatives to SWOT. This strategic planning tool can provide the masjid with a clear idea of what issues need to be addressed and the appropriate direction for the masjid's future. This allows masjid administrators to leverage their strengths and opportunities, and learn from and prepare for weaknesses and threats. Once the analysis is completed, the administrators can develop a strategic plan, after which they should also prepare an annual calendar of activities.

It is the duty of the board to annually review the performance of the Executive Director or the CEO. After the review, the board should also provide guidance and direction to the executives on an annual basis.

The budget is the financial picture of what the masjid hopes to accomplish over the year. For many masjid administrators the budget is the most uncomfortable part of leadership. It does not need to be painful. At its core, the budgeting process is planning. It provides the administrators an opportunity to reflect on what they have accomplished last year and what they wish to accomplish the next year. The budget is essentially a financial plan that answers the following question: "What funds do we need to spend to accomplish our goals?" Once developed, the board should formally approve the budget. The approved budget then document becomes the guideline for spending for the next year.[1]

Donor Relationship Management

Like all nonprofits, masjids rely on donors to get established and to keep operating. Masjids should keep donors engaged and let them know that they're part of the team. This requires a lot of work.

The key to keeping donors invested in the masjid is to help them feel included. This can be done by involving them in making decisions and reminding them that they are integral parts of the masjid. It is also important to thank them for their support, as the Messenger of Allah ﷺ taught us that "whoever does not thank the people does not thank Allah" (Tirmidhi – Sahih)

Another important element to masjid-donor relations is transparency. Supporters will be more trusting when you tell them how their money was spent. This can be done with a simple periodic report every year or every quarter. Building a relationship with the community that is based on trust and mutual respect will help promote future donations and support.

Financial Sustainability

Once the masjid is built, we also have to find ways to ensure its long term financial sustainability. In classical times, the masjid was typically accompanied by a *waqf* to support the masjid financially. This was accomplished by Muslims donating land to the masjid that would be farmed to produce income for the masjid. Nowadays, it is very common in Muslim countries for a masjid to be attached to a storefront, or an integrated shopping complex, where stores pay rent to the masjid.

Masjid administrators should try to establish a long term financial sustainability plan for the masjid. Ideas for financial sustainability include establishing an endowment fund or foundation, investing in businesses for the masjid, purchasing rental opportunities, and acquiring other revenue streams. We have to encourage Muslim donors to help setup endowments and revenue streams for the masjid.

1 Nonprofit Budgeting. Part 1: Budget Basics. CompassPoint Nonprofit Services. 2017 (URL: https://www.compasspoint.org/sites/default/files/documents/Nonprofit%20Budgeting%20I%20-%20Budget%20Basics%20Manual.pdf)

Overhead Costs

It is the duty of the masjid to spend the funds it receives on the programs and services for the community. Many masjid administrators mistakenly think that administrative expenses should be zero or very low. But administrators are essential to properly operate any institution. In recognition of this reality, Allah the Exalted made a provision in zakat expenditures for those who administer the zakat:

إِنَّمَا ٱلصَّدَقَٰتُ لِلْفُقَرَآءِ وَٱلْمَسَٰكِينِ وَٱلْعَٰمِلِينَ عَلَيْهَا وَٱلْمُؤَلَّفَةِ قُلُوبُهُمْ وَفِى ٱلرِّقَابِ وَٱلْغَٰرِمِينَ وَفِى سَبِيلِ ٱللَّهِ وَٱبْنِ ٱلسَّبِيلِ فَرِيضَةً مِّنَ ٱللَّهِ وَٱللَّهُ عَلِيمٌ حَكِيمٌ

Indeed, the charity is only to be spent upon the poor and the indigent, and to those who work on administering it, and to those whose hearts are to be reconciled, and to free slaves, and to the debt-ridden, and for the cause of God, and to the traveler. This is an obligation from God. And God is all-knowing, all-wise. (*Qur'an 9:60*)

Masjid administrators need to strike a balance. Insufficient administrative expenditures will hinder the quality, sustainability, and proper delivery of the programs and services of the masjid, while too much overhead and administrative expenditures would reduce the programs and services that the masjid can deliver. We recommend that 65-80 percent of total expenses (not total income) be spent on program services. We also recommend that masjids start saving funds in an endowment fund for long term sustainability.

Can Zakat Be Used For The masjid?

Since classical times, religious scholars have ruled that it is not permissible to use Zakat money for the purpose of building, maintaining or expanding a masjid in a Muslim country. The underlying logic is that establishing the ṣalāh is the duty of the Ummah. Since masjids are necessary to establish ṣalāh, the Ummah has an affirmative duty to establish masjids. This duty of establishing ṣalāh has historically been held to be a duty independent of the duty to pay zakat. Modern ulema generally agree with classical ulema on the impermissibility of using zakat funds for the purpose of building, maintaining, or expanding a masjid in a country with a majority Muslim population.

In 1405 AH/1983 CE, the International Islamic Fiqh Academy of the Muslim World League issued a verdict regarding Muslims who live as minorities. They reasoned that in countries where Muslims are minorities, the masjids are centers of daʿwah, engaging in the propagation of Islam "in the path of Allah." One of the eight categories delineated in the Qur'an for zakat expenditures is "*fi sabeel illah*," in the path of Allah. Thus they considered building masjids in non-Muslim countries to be a valid expense under this category of zakat.[2]

In 1437 AH/2015 CE the American Muslim Jurists Association (AMJA) issued a statement at the end of their 12th conference. It took a more reserved position, holding it permissible to use zakat funds to build masjids in non-Muslim countries only if other funds proved insufficient for building masjids where they are needed. They clarified it would be a valid expense under the fi sabeel illah category of zakat. It further clarified that paying off the debt of a masjid would also qualify under the "relieving the debts" category of zakat.[3]

Religious Land Use & Institutionalized Persons Act (RLUIPA)

(The statements in this section only apply to masjids in the United States of America. Masjids in other countries should consult their specific legal regulations)

We previously discussed the opposition and hatred of Islam. One specific mechanism of Islamophobia is to mount heated opposition to the approval of zoning and construction permits for new masjids. In most cases their opposition is cloaked in technical arguments such as concern about increased traffic or safety issues. Across the United States, city councils and planning boards frequently surrender to severe public pressure by denying the necessary approvals or construction permits. As a result the Muslim communities often spend many years and a lot of money before succeeding in building a new masjid.

The Religious Land Use & Institutionalized Persons Act (RLUIPA) addresses this problem:

> RLUIPA prohibits a local government from imposing or implementing a land use regulation, defined specifically in the act as zoning and landmarking, in any way that imposes a substantial burden on the free exercise of individuals or a religious assembly or institution, unless the government can demonstrate that it (1) has a compelling interest to justify the regulation,

2 Salah Assawi. صرف الزكاة فى أعمال التعليم والدعوة Zakat Expenditures For Education And Dawah. Fatawaalsawy.com. 2017 (URL: http://fatawaalsawy.com/الفقه/العبادات/الزكاة/صرف-الزكاة-في-أعمال-التعليم-والدعوة/)

3 AMJA 12th Imam Conference. Recommendations of the Conference on Contemporary Issues Facing Islamic Centers in the West. American Muslim Jurists Association. 2015. (URL: http://www.amjaonline.org/en/component/content/article/19-imams-conference/98-amja-12th-imams-conference)

and (2) has used the least restrictive means to achieve that interest. Under RLUIPA, the bar that a government body must meet to consider a zoning or landmarking action more compelling than free religious practice is high. It must be reached in a rational, fact-based process that is demonstrably unbiased and fair.

There are two key aspects of RLUIPA that faith communities should understand. First, the act requires local, state and federal bodies to treat religious assemblies on equal terms with nonreligious assemblies (such as private clubs or lodges). That is, religious assemblies may not be excluded where secular assemblies are permitted, and they must be given the same zoning rights. Second, as written, RLUIPA considers accessory functions (such as affiliated schools, food pantries, senior centers, cemeteries, and the like) essential to the free exercise of religion and calls for them to be regulated in the same way that the primary worship spaces are regulated. That is, a local government may not place a substantial burden on the accessory use, either.[4]

We urge administrators of organizations seeking to establish a new masjid to familiarize themselves with this law and how it might impact them.

Political Activities in the Masjid

(The statements in this section only apply to masjids in the United States of America. Masjids in other countries should consult their specific legal regulations)

Due to the rise of Islamophobia, the Muslim community urgently needs to arise and claim its political power. It is the masjid's duty to facilitate this effort for the Muslim community.

Contrary to popular belief, masjids are not prohibited from engaging in political activities; they are only prohibited from engaging in campaigning. The differences are subtle but important.

Permitted political activities include but are not limited to:

- Voter registration drives
- Non-partisan candidate debates
- Non-partisan voter education
- Legislative advocacy
- Issue advocacy
- Lobbying activities less than 10% of annual expenditures

4 Kathleen E. Foley. Building Mosques In America: Strategies for Securing Municipal Approvals. Institute for Social Policy and Understanding. October 2010 (URL: https://www.ispu.org/wp-content/uploads/2016/08/ISPU_Building_Mosques_Report.pdf)

- Permitting candidates for an elected office to speak at the masjid provided all candidates for the same elected office are given the same or similar opportunities to speak

Prohibited political campaigning includes but is not limited to:

- Inviting only one political candidate to make a campaign speech
- Endorsing or opposing a candidate on the masjid's website
- Using masjid funds to publish materials that support (or oppose) a candidate
- Donating money from the masjid to a political candidate
- Conducting a partisan "get out the vote" telephone drive to promote a particular candidate

Any individuals associated with the masjid (including the Imam and Executive Director) are entitled to voice their opinions and participate in a political campaign, as long as they are not speaking for the masjid during their political work.

Insurance Coverage

Insurance is a must in today's environment. In the past decade, masjids have been burned to the ground by Islamophobes, sued for slips in the parking lot, and severely damaged by natural weather such as hurricanes & earthquakes. It is a risk for a masjid to forgo proper insurance coverage that would protect them against unforeseen circumstances. A million dollars of damage could easily have been protected with a few thousand dollars in insurance premiums.

There are several types of insurance policies:

General Property Insurance covers losses and damages to the land, building and items inside the property of the masjid. We recommend each masjid to maintain property insurance at all times for 120% of the replacement value of the masjid. If the masjid was built 15 years ago for 1 million dollars, but we estimate that it would cost 4 million dollars to build a similar masjid today, then the masjid should maintain property insurance in the amount of 4.8 million dollars.

General Liability Insurance covers injuries that the masjid (or its leadership, employees or agents) cause to third parties. If someone sues the masjid for personal harm or property damage, the cost of defending and resolving the suit would be covered by the liability insurance policy.

Errors and Omissions Insurance covers the masjid (or its leadership, employees, or agents) for any inadvertent mistakes or failures that caused injury to a third party. The action must actually be an inadvertent error, and not merely poor judgment or intentional acts.

Directors and Officers Liability Insurance covers claims made against the directors and officers of the masjid for actions they undertake on behalf of the masjid.

Umbrella Insurance increases business liability protection when the costs of a lawsuit exceed the limits of the primary underlying business liability coverage.

Most masjids are able to purchase a combination of the above in the form of a **Business Owners Policy**, or BOP. This is typically done for the masjid to receive a customized policy tailored to the specific needs of the masjid.

Conclusion

The administration of a masjid is a complex matter with many aspects. To that end, we recommend that masjids should:

- Hold monthly board meetings
- Review monthly financial statements
- Establish an annual board work plan
- Perform a SWOT analysis and strategic plan
- Adopt an annual calendar of activities before each year
- Annually provide executive leadership a review of their performance
- Adopt a budget before the beginning of each year, use it as a guide for the whole year, and report against the budget to reconcile differences
- Actively manage donor relationships
- Establish an endowment for the masjid
- 65-80 percent of total expenses (not total income) should be spent on program services
- Familiarize themselves with how RLUIPA affects the masjid
- Engage in permitted political activities to benefit the Muslim community while avoiding prohibited political campaigning
- Purchase a combined Business Owners Policy (BOP), that includes General Property, General Liability, Errors and Omissions Insurance, Directors and Officers Liability, Umbrella Insurance Policy
- Purchase property insurance at all times for 120% of the replacement value

Chapter 14: Survey Results

We urge masjid administrators to regularly solicit feedback from the community. Allah the Exalted describes the believers as follows.

وَٱلَّذِينَ ٱسْتَجَابُوا لِرَبِّهِمْ وَأَقَامُوا ٱلصَّلَوٰةَ وَأَمْرُهُمْ شُورَىٰ بَيْنَهُمْ
وَمِمَّا رَزَقْنَٰهُمْ يُنفِقُونَ

"And those who responded to their Lord and established ṣalāh and determined affairs by consultation among themselves, and spend from what We have provided them." (*Qur'an 42:38*)

In this chapter, we provide a few selected comments from various focus groups about masjid Best Practices. These provide a glimpse of how our work impacts the people we serve.

Focus Group #1: 5 women leaders of community or social service programs (*Free form comments*)

- The Muslim community appears to be satisfied with mediocrity. We are not holding our masjid to high standards. We don't know how to ask for better practices from our masjids.
- Masjids are not relevant for the current society that we are living in. masjids should maximize the opportunities and rise to the challenges.
- Masjids need to have diverse boards. Most masjids don't have any youth or women on their boards. Most boards are not ethnically diverse.
- Women help in many areas of the masjid but are not visible in the masjid nor on the board.
- Sisters should be speakers in the masjid.
- A good masjid should have a vibrant study circle for women.
- Bringing in the community is the priority. Fatwas, and labelling are pushing people away from masjids.
- Invite speakers from different groups and viewpoints in the masjid.
- Get involved in the media.
- Board members need to get training.
- Masjids need to go back to the original model of the Rasul ﷺ
- Are the youth allowed to freely participate in the masjid, or are they locked in the closet?
- Does the masjid have a culture that children are not welcome?
- Youth energy is blocked. If youth are not part of the "group", then they are not allowed to do events.

- Welcoming environment
- Masjids should provide youth mentors
- Masjid leaders have a personal relationship with the elected officials
- Respect scholars and lay people equally so we recognize what each group brings to the table
- Proper recruitment of board members based on skills, voice and perspective based on inclusivity
- We need green masjids which promote recycling, stop using Styrofoam, restrict water bottle usage and install energy efficient appliances/ light bulbs

Focus Group #2: 11 girls and 9 boys between the ages of nine and eighteen. (Five questions were asked)

1. Please describe something good that happened to you in a masjid.
- 75% of youth can think of something happy in a masjid.
- I enjoy Iftar parties.
- I enjoy carnivals.
- I enjoy games & entertainment.
- Someone I dislike was yelled at.
- It was my first time in a masjid, someone welcomed me, introduced me and offered me a ride.
- I enjoy playing with little kids in the masjid.
- I enjoy tea after taraweeḥ.
- I enjoy playing basketball at the masjid.
- The masjid had proper accommodations for women.

2. Please describe something bad that happened to you in a masjid.
- People were smoking outside the masjid door.
- Long and boring sermons
- Getting yelled at
- I dislike being forced to volunteer to set up for Iftar.
- I was chased by an old man through the alley.
- Fundraising on the 27th night in the middle of ṣalāh
- Someone borrowed my shoes to go to the bathroom.
- Unclean bathrooms
- Someone threw away my toys.
- There was no room on the shoe rack.
- No parking/ inconsiderate parking/ disorganized parking
- Loud kids during ṣalāh
- Angry uncles
- Imam yelled at me because I was wearing shorts to jumah.

3. Think of the masjid administrator (imam, board member, youth co-ordinator) whom you like the best. Tell us why you like this person the most.

- He plays with kids.
- He is young and understands kids.
- He makes learning fun.
- He is entertaining.
- He is easy to understand.

4. Tell us what the masjid facilities should be like

- Clean
- Separation between screaming kids and the rest of the youth
- Smell good
- Air conditioning
- masjid should be close to my home
- Clean the stinky carpet
- Modern feel
- Open layout
- Spacious room for the women to pray, not a cramped space
- Spacious rooms
- Remove the bugs
- Good smelling bathrooms
- Attractive masjid
- Water fountains where the water does not taste stale

5. If your masjid had extra money, what would you spend it on?

- Basketball court
- Parking lot
- iPads
- Decorations
- Public classes
- Library
- Air fresheners
- English translations of the Qur'an
- Open places to eat
- Social programs
- Better quality bathrooms
- Exterminator
- Extra hijabs for women who show up without a hijab
- Proper wudu'station
- Dry floors in the bathrooms